ENCOUNTER
WITH DISASTER

Col. Ashley W. Oughterson

Lt. Col. Averill A. Liebow

Prof. Masao Tsuzuki

ENCOUNTER WITH DISASTER

A Medical Diary of Hiroshima,

1945

AVERILL A. LIEBOW

W · W · NORTON & COMPANY · INC ·

NEW YORK

To
Carolyn B. Gott–L.,
who waited

Contents

Acknowledgments

Although Japanese medical investigating teams had been at work in Hiroshima within three days of the atomic bombing, and although a brief survey had been made between September 8 and 19, 1945, by a team under Col. Stafford L. Warren, representing the "Manhattan District," the responsibility for a comprehensive medical study was placed on the Joint Commission for the Investigation of the Effects of the Atomic Bomb in Japan. The timely organization of the Commission was the work of Col. Ashley W. Oughterson, surgical consultant in the Pacific Theatre of Operations. It was accomplished in the field, since no thoroughgoing preparations had been made in Washington. It was of necessity impromptu, the personnel assigned were not specially prepared, and there was no equipment in hand.

This diary provides a record of how the Joint Commission was formed, of the establishment of the essential working relationship with Japanese medical investigators immediately after the cessation of hostilities, and of the trials and rewards of daily activities during stressful times from September 18 to December 6, 1945. There is also a short account of the preparation of the report at the Army Institute of Pathology, to the time of its completion on September 7, 1946. At the hazard of disturbing continuity, explanatory notes enclosed in brackets have been put into the text. These provide background without which the bare daily record might be less than fully comprehensible.

Illustrative material was drawn in large part from the original report of the Joint Commission. The writer wishes to express his appreciation to Brig. Gen. Joe M. Blumberg, the director of the Armed Forces Institute of Pathology, for making this material available. Most of it has never been published. All of the early photographs that were incorporated into this report were made by Japanese investigators or news agencies. One of the first on the scene and among the most observant of the investigators was Professor Nishina, the famous physicist. Personnel of the Tokyo Dai Ichi Military Hospital supplied graphic illustrations of patients at the height of the aplastic anemia. Photographs by the Bunka-Sha Agency of medical activities at Hiroshima prior to the arrival of the Commission are noteworthy for their technical excellence. Particular credit is due to Capt. Charles Brownell and his staff, members of the Joint Commission, who were highly skilled, sensitive to the medical and human problems, and tireless workers. Last and least are personal photographs made by the writer during the time covered by the diary, and again in 1949 on another visit to Hiroshima. These provided an opportunity to see the city in renascence. Two of the color plates were first published in *Medical Radiography and Photography* (Eastman Kodak Company), Volume 24, No. 2, 1948. These were prepared in part from personal 35-mm. transparencies and in part from larger transparencies made by Captain Brownell. Permission to use these was graciously given by the editor, Mr. William Cornwell. The McGraw-Hill Book Company also permitted the use of several diagrams and sketches reproduced from the original report of the Joint Commission in *Medical Effects of the Atomic Bomb in Japan* (A. W. Oughterson and S. Warren, eds., 1956).

Men of the Yale Medical School were closely associated with the studies at Hiroshima from the beginning and have remained so to the present time. Colonel Oughterson himself was an associate professor of surgery on leave, and three others of the seven medical officers assigned to Hiroshima had been Yale medical students and two were on leave from the faculty. After the Atomic Bomb Casualty Commission (ABCC) was established in 1948, one of the first pathologists assigned was Dr. William J. Wedemeyer. A major contribution was made by another former Yale medical student, Dr. Thomas Francis, Jr., late professor of public health at the University of Michigan, who designed the closed-population sampling study that is now the core of the operation at ABCC. Since 1957 the ABCC has been under the distinguished directorship of Dr. George B.

Darling, professor of human ecology at Yale. Finally, both able personnel and an important degree of continuity have been assured by the assumption of responsibility for the medical service at Hiroshima since 1958 by the Department of Internal Medicine at Yale. For these reasons it is appropriate that this diary was first published in *The Yale Journal of Biology and Medicine*. The original diary and much of the documentary material are stored in the historical library of the Yale University School of Medicine.

Introduction

Among the myriad words written about the atomic bombing at Hiroshima and Nagasaki, there are few records that are basic and contemporary. Some, such as the brief and stark description of the Hiroshima bombing by Father Siemes, present the viewpoint of a lay eyewitness; others, such as the report of the U.S. Strategic Bombing Survey, present cold and appalling facts. Still other accounts, such as John Hersey's *Hiroshima*, provide a vivid, imaginative record in which artistry necessarily rules, but without major distortions of substance. In the twenty-five years that have passed since the event, facts tend to be blurred by emotion, history by loss of full and accurate detail.

Dr. Liebow has given an important, detailed presentation of the grim aftermath of the bombing at Hiroshima as seen by the keen eye of a disciplined observer, tempered by the knowledge and warmth of a skilled physician. A key member of the medical investigative teams, he lets us share in the desperate efforts to help those all too often beyond help, the urgent push for knowledge about how better to aid the victims of an unprecedented cataclysm, the harrassment and frustrations incident to lack of equipment and supplies. Thanks to his skill at shorthand, Dr. Liebow was able to record each night the wealth of his experiences, his concern for mankind as a physician and moralist, and his reactions to an alien culture. We can see the improvised hospitals and laboratories, smell the results of the breakdown of most civic functions, touch the shoddy dressings or see the raw major wounds and burns of the survivors.

As one who shared experiences with him, although my work was chiefly in Nagasaki, I know the burden of concern for the patients, the responsibilities of the medical officer for his men and fellow officers. Dr. Liebow helps us feel in greater and greater detail the realization of the potential doom that man had created for himself in the atomic bombs.

This detailed account makes vivid also the international character of medicine and the ability of doctors from enemy countries to work together for the benefit of their patients in spite of dissimilar cultures and philosophies of life and the confusion of different languages. Dr. Liebow's outgoing personality and experience as a teacher helped greatly in laying the foundation for international cooperation in the study and help of the Hiroshima-Nagasaki survivors that soon eventuated in the establishment of the Atomic Bomb Casualty Commission. This joint enterprise of the Japanese and United States governments is continuing to function and to reap for mankind much fruitful information from work with the survivors. For years Dr. Liebow has served as an advisor to the National Academy of Sciences in its operation of the Atomic Bomb Casualty Commission. Not only did he play an important role in the pioneering studies outlined here, but he also co-authored the definitive treatise on the injurious effects of the atomic bomb on man.

Shields Warren, M.D.

December 24, 1969

ENCOUNTER
WITH DISASTER

CHAPTER 1

Why and How

For twenty years, while the seven rivers that meander into Hiroshima Bay have lapped upon the shores of a reviving city, this diary has remained in the shorthand in which it was set down. The writing was done at the end of each arduous day before and during the medical investigation in that stricken city, often in exhaustion. Some who have known of it have urged that it would be wrong that such a record, workaday as it is, should be permitted to dissolve with the flesh. Let us hope that the experience which it reports will remain unique! It is true that few who took part are left to tell how the challenge was met and what took place. Indeed it is as though some curse, like that which the superstitious say fell upon Lord Carnarvon and his men when they violated the tomb of Pharaoh Tut-ankhamen, has been visited upon those who pried into the ravaged heart of Hiroshima. Only three of the seven American medical officers live. Drs. Oughterson and Tsuzuki, the chief organizers for the two countries, have died; so too, while still young, have Drs. Calvin Koch, Jack D. Rosenbaum, and Milton R. Kramer. May this record do honor to these able and devoted men.

It was not through a *horror scribendi* that these notes have languished. Rather it was through fear that some insignificant phrase might be misconstrued in a way that could disturb the amity that has grown between Japan and America, and specifically the continuing cooperation in the Atomic Bomb Casualty Commission. Too many of the wicked have been all too eager to distort in order to disrupt!

Those of us who came to Hiroshima in September 1945 soon acquired a profound admiration and respect for our Japanese counterparts. We knew that the medical study could not be accomplished without knowledge of the language, people, and customs. We knew also that many skilled men would be needed since the few of us who had been sent represented only a smattering of the specialties. It is a tribute to the vision and humanity of Col. Ashley W. Oughterson, truly a man without malice, that the collaboration of Japanese science and medicine was invited at that critical time. We called ourselves the "Joint Commission for the Investigation of the Effects of the Atomic Bomb in Japan." As soon as the Japanese discovered that the word "Joint" meant that both nations were to labor shoulder to shoulder to meet the formidable task of the medical study, and that they would be treated not as enemies vanquished, but rather as colleagues and equals, they gave unstintingly of their thought and labor. The friendships that began then have grown to a firmness that will resist calumny.

My own involvement was a matter of being at hand when the circumstance created the need. I was serving on the island of Saipan in the Marianas, in my third year as pathologist to the Thirty-ninth General Hospital, the Yale Unit. In early 1945 peaks of effort were required to care for casualties of the Okinawa and Iwo Jima campaigns, but there were quiet intervals when scientific hobbies such as the study of cutaneous diphtheria could be indulged among the interesting, intelligent, and tractable native population. The contemplation of nature in the lush green jungle or even in the sugar cane was dangerous. Although the island was declared "secure," these were the hiding places of Japanese soldiers wishing to be left alone but likely to ambush intruders. Each evening we watched fleets of B-29 bombers making a rendezvous with their kind from neighboring Tinian and Guam to carry death and destruction to Iwo and Japan. As with full loads they lumbered straining to the end of the runway, many would actually drop below the level of the cliff that overhung the reef at land's end. A few did crash into the sea, and some would jettison their bombs and circle back to the landing strip. As we lounged on the terrace overlooking the cobalt of Magicienne Bay, we felt the guilt of insufficient involvement. This grew when the planes returned in the morning, some limping and with a cargo of injured or dead, or when we learned of those that never came back.

Of the existence of an atomic bomb we had no inkling. It is true that in the spring of 1945 wagers that the war would end by August 15 were being freely made by airmen who, with enigmatic smiles, even offered substantial odds. Yet the actual secret was well kept. Enormous casings shaped like bombs were being dragged on multi-wheeled flat carriers over the hot, white, dusty, coral roads of Saipan, but these were undoubtedly decoys, and none of the bettors knew more than that something great and terrible was in the wind. Only a few had knowledge of the awesome power that lay in a low, closely guarded, concrete, windowless building on the Island of Tinian, only three miles from us across the water.

Even as Iwo Jima, the last steppingstone to Japan, was being seized, and before Tinian received its fateful burden, we were busily expanding our unit to 2,000 beds. We were not alone. Vast new hospitals were rising on Tinian and Guam. Together we were to serve as a great center to receive casualties from the expected assault on the Japanese homeland.

When, at 8:14 on the morning of August 6, 1945, on command from Washington, the hand aboard the *Enola Gay* loosed beyond recall a new evil in the world, we had no knowledge of how our lives, in fact the lives of all men, would be changed. Only three days later came the second devastating blow, against Nagasaki, before we on Saipan knew of the first. No further conviction was required.

I can well remember how the news of peace came to us. It was on the evening of August 11, 1945. My wife to be and I were at cribbage in the Officers' Club. Two befuddled marines were consoling themselves by idly twirling the dials of a short-wave radio when Carolyn suddenly exclaimed: "Did you hear that? They want peace." I had not heard. We rushed to the set, but by then the station had been lost and we spent the next half hour searching. Finally it came. Personal bottles were rescued from the bar, since the commanding officer's orders required that it be closed at 11:00 P.M. Then followed a snake-dance to announce the news to all and sundry in the barracks; it continued past the startled sentries of the fenced-off nurses' compound. All was uproar and gaiety throughout the night, assisted by a supply of Scotch with which the chief nurse had been entrusted by one of the generals. On the next day destroyer-escorts equipped with blaring loudspeakers cruised along the coast and shouted the news in Japanese into every inlet. They were believed, or else confirmed by more direct sources from Tokyo, since within the week no fewer than 400 of the erstwhile enemy turned themselves in. They had successfully managed to elude several mopping-up operations. Most were neither sick nor thin. Many had continued to feast, as had we when we first arrived, on tinned crabmeat made in Japan, which bore the label "Approved by *Good Housekeeping*." This had been cached in caves before the battle for the island.

Now came the time to discharge our few patients either back to duty or to hospitals near home, and to release those of our staff who had sufficient "points." The necessary quota applied to most of us who had been with the unit from the time it was organized. Since facilities for transportation were obviously limited I elected to remain for two reasons. First, others had wives and young families at home; second, as historian to the Yale Unit, I wished to record the last events in the closing, and particularly the destruction of the equipment, the return of which to the homeland had been proscribed. Had permission not been granted to remain, I would probably have been ordered back from some point on the long journey home. As it was, the orders caught me unaware and unprepared, but not physically on the homing path, and therefore ready, in fact eager, to set forth on the final step to Japan that we had begun more than three years before.

CHAPTER 2

Hiroshima Retrospect

Hiroshima, "broad island," is really a delta cut into six islands by the branches of the River Ota. Here lived some 250,000 people, a number that does not include the soldiers of the Chugoku Army in their encampment near the center. On two sides of the delta, which points its apex to the north, the hills rise sharply. It is as if a great flatiron had been pressed from the direction of the sea into the mountains. Only the truncated cone of Hijiyama rising to 225 feet interrupts the flatness.

For the most part the houses were of traditional Japanese construction. Most were of one or two stories, built of wooden lathwork and clay. A central heavy tree beam ran longitudinally, supporting arch-like ties. These in turn supported a lattice of struts that braced the heavy roof of overlapping pantiles. Most of the modern buildings were of the heavy construction necessitated in this land of earthquakes. These were situated along the main street at the southern boundary of the military encampment and also along the broad thoroughfare, which ran at right angles directly south from the main entrance of the reservation. These buildings were not in a cluster, but separated by rows of the wooden shops and dwellings. Buildings of weight-bearing brick were few, since these are most subject to damage by earthquake. Typical Japanese cities built thus tend to be

Air strips on Tinian used for B-29 bombers. From this island the bomber *Enola Gay* carried the bomb that destroyed Hiroshima.

swept by disastrous fires at an average interval of eight years, but the ordinary houses, quick to burn, can be as quickly rebuilt. The open charcoal braziers (*hibachi*) useful for warmth and for cooking are a constant hazard. In this city of islands the branches of the Ota made natural fire breaks, but the separate islands were themselves large and densely crowded. In recognition of the danger of fire, especially under air attack, the citizens even before April 1945 had organized patriotic work parties (*giyutai*) to create additional firebreaks by leveling blocks of homes. Work parties for this purpose were also recruited from outlying villages such as Otake.

Hiroshima was not an important center of industry. On the outskirts were a branch of Toyo Industries, Mitsubishi shipyards, and a machine-tool factory. The Japan Steel Company was to the northeast. There were also two large rayon plants, one located at Ujina on the far end of the easternmost island near the harbor. It was here that patients were later brought under care of the Tokyo First (Dai Ichi) Military Hospital and that we were to establish the headquarters for our work. Industry was also scattered in innumerable home workshops, in accordance with the Japanese concept of total war.

In Hiroshima, in a roughly pentagonal area near the center of the city, was concentrated the military power of central Japan. The headquarters of the Second Grand Army and of the Chugoku military district were located near an ornate castle, a relic of the Tokugawas, on an artificial island surrounded by a moat. Near the southwestern part of the pentagon were divisional headquarters and barracks, row on row. Near the entrance of the encampment, facing the boulevard at its southern border, was the impressive Gokoku shrine. The Hiroshima encampment had served as the springboard for the conquest

A rare aerial view of Hiroshima before 1945. This was a restricted military area, and photography had been forbidden since 1937. The view corresponds to the northern half of the island with the white, apron-like extension seen in the lower photograph.

Hiroshima—a post-strike view. The inner white circle is drawn at 500 meters around the hypocenter and the outer at 1,000. The black line indicates the zone of total destruction, chiefly by fire. This extends 2,000 to 2,300 meters from the hypocenter and is delimited in part by natural firebreaks. The numbers indicate the buildings used in the shielding study: No. 11, Chugoku Electric Company; No. 211, Chugoku army headquarters, communications trench; No. 61, broadcasting station JOFK; No. 28, City Hall; No. 65, Communications Department; No. 31, Red Cross Hospital.

of Manchuria in 1937–45, and before that for the successful attack on Port Arthur. Of late, the military importance of this center had waned, and it was largely serving the function of a quartermaster depot. Ordnance and munitions were stored in caves along the road leading to the naval bases of Kure to the north and Iwakuni to the south.

In a military sense, at least the army base might be considered a legitimate target, yet it was strange that before August 1945 Hiroshima had escaped almost unharmed. Desultory raids between the middle of March and April 30, 1945, had inflicted almost no damage. During the early summer our propaganda had broadcast threats that a number of cities, including Hiroshima, would be destroyed. The population was tense with expectation. Yet on August 6, the element of surprise was complete. Four B-29 bombers were sighted over Hiroshima early in the morning, but shortly after 7:00 A.M. they withdrew to the northwest. Just after 8:00 three planes returned, but the all-clear had sounded forty-five minutes before. Since there was no large concentration of hostile aircraft, the people went about their business as they had been told to do. At that moment Hiroshima was a city going to work. Farmers were already in the fields on the outskirts of the city. The streets were filled. Children had already reported to the schools or for service in clearing firebreaks. Customers had arrived in the banks but had not as yet been admitted to the floor. It was a time when the hazard of direct exposure in the open was close to its peak. One of the planes was seen to release several objects by parachute, and then at 8:14, despite the brightness of the morning, survivors were startled by a prolonged and brilliant flash, like that of a gigantic magnesium flare. Accompanying the flash of light was an instantaneous flash of heat traveling with the speed of light and perceptible as far away as Ninoshima, the beautiful conical island five miles across Hiroshima Bay. The heat affected exposed objects with an intensity inversely proportional to the square of the distance from the epicenter. Its duration was probably less than one-tenth of a second, and its intensity was sufficient to cause nearby flammable objects, particularly when dark, to burst into flame and to char poles as far as 4,000 yards away from the hypocenter (the point directly beneath the center of the explosion). At 600 to 700 yards it was sufficient to chip and roughen granite by unequal expansion of its components. The heat also produced bubbling of tile to about 1,300 yards. It has been found by experiment that to produce this effect a temperature of 1,800° C. acting for four seconds is necessary, but under these conditions the effect is deeper, which indicates that the temperature was higher and the duration less during the Hiroshima explosion. Only surfaces directly exposed sustained flash burns, since rays of heat, like light, travel in straight lines. Intervening objects prevented the charring or other alteration in the directly exposed surfaces and thereby cast "shadows." The sharpness of shadows cast by constantly moving objects like leaves also suggests the brief duration of the flash. Thousands of persons in the open within a radius of two-and-a-half miles sustained more-or-less severe flash burns, depending on distance and the protective effect of clothing.

After an interval evident to those at a distance, there came a violent shock wave that flattened the fragile wooden buildings. As seen from the hills, the houses fell as under a scythe. People were hurled from where they were standing. Those closest by heard almost no sound except for that of falling buildings, but at a distance there was a rumbling roar like that of thunder. The blast wave shot outwards at approximately two miles per second for a relatively short distance but then after several hundred yards reached the speed of sound (approximately 1,100 feet per second). It rose to a sharp peak, and then the pressure fell below atmospheric for a period perhaps three times that of the positive phase. Objects at a distance were deflected away from the center of the blast, but such objects as trees immediately beneath remained standing upright although stripped of their branches. The magnitude of the downward pressure was shown by the "dishing" of the reinforced concrete roofs of buildings. Glass and other debris were shot through the air like bullets, often became impacted in wood, and inflicted multiple serious injuries. Simultaneously, a roiling cloud, pink or black according to various observers, rose from the point of the explosion; this, together with immense quantities of dust from the ground and from the collapsing buildings, threw those beneath it into almost total darkness that lasted for some twenty minutes. Thousands were trapped in the wreckage. Almost all of those who could not escape under their own power perished. Fires, beginning everywhere both by direct ignition and by the upsetting of thousands of the open *hibachi*, many still in use for cooking breakfast, at once swept the city. A high wind sucked toward the rising atomic cloud fanned the flames, which then created their

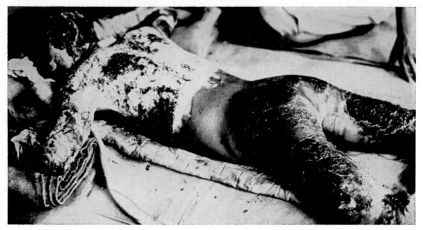

A flash burn in the acute stage; the upper portion of the body was un-
clothed and suffered a sharply outlined profile burn. The patient was
probably within 1,000 meters of the hypocenter. The buttocks and thighs
were burned through the clothing, but the abdomen was protected by
a multi-layered cummerbund.

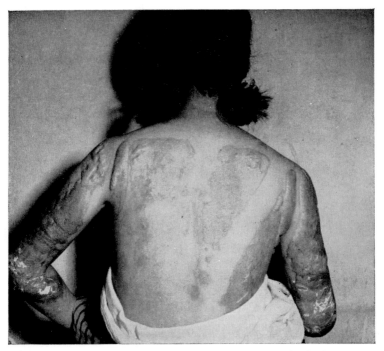

Keloids on the skin of a twenty-one-year-old woman who had been 1,600
meters from the hypocenter, seen in early November 1945. Some protection was provided by a blouse and the straps of undergarments.

own fire storm. The victims suffered burns both by flash and by flame.

As soon as the atomic nature of the explosion was announced a new fear made itself felt—the terror of the invisible. The existence of radiation effects was known almost at once. People who had been close to the hypocenter but who had suffered neither burns nor trauma sickened and died. They felt weak and nauseated, could not eat, and developed severe diarrhea and fever; some died within ten days. Those who survived longer lost their hair; hemorrhages and ulcers appeared in the skin and mucous membranes, and death resulted from pulmonary or intestinal infections. The marrow had been destroyed, and all elements of the blood were depleted.

If the intent of the bombing was demoralization, this was unquestionably achieved. False rumors spread—that all who had been in Hiroshima and Nagasaki would die, and that the cities would be uninhabitable for seventy-five years. But there was yet another effect. Those in power in Japan who were wise had clearly seen that the war had been lost when Okinawa and Iwo Jima fell. The emperor had personally sought to influence his war councilors to sue for peace. Now, in the face of unanticipated and unprecedented power that could overwhelm even the most valorous, there was a way to conclude the war without losing face—and the fighting was brought to an end.

Only glimpses can be obtained from accounts of survivors of the immense medical problems created by an atomic explosion in a densely populated city. Those who lived were dazed not merely by the immediate force of the explosion but by its vast extent. Many lost consciousness for a few seconds or minutes even though they had not suffered trauma to the head. Darkness interrupted by onrushing fires added to the confusion and terror. No one knew which way to escape. The riverbanks and their waters were natural havens, and were soon teeming. Boats were mobilized to carry survivors upstream. Only a few could be brought out on litters or carts, and almost all who could not rescue themselves were overwhelmed by the flames. Both administrative authority and organized activity had ceased to exist. What was done was done on individual initiative. Only three of forty-five hospitals in the city remained standing. The two largest and most modern, the Red Cross Hospital and the Communications Department (Post Office) Hospital, were so severely damaged by blast, as was their equipment, that they could function only as first-aid stations. Fewer than 10 per cent of the city's 300 physicians were uninjured, and nursing strength had been equally depleted.

As the fires cooled relief work was begun. The first relief station from outside was set up on the afternoon of August 6 at Tamon, in the shelter of Hijiyama. Thousands streamed back into the city in search of relatives and friends. Messages were scrawled on the walls of the aid stations. Police control, by tradition an enveloping power in Japan, was resumed with the help of officers from neighboring towns. The armed forces gave substantial aid. Two relief parties were dispatched from the Naval base at nearby Kure, and the hospital on the base at Iwakuni received fifty-one patients, many of whom were naval personnel who had been quartered at the Bankers' Club, a large building only 200 yards from the hypocenter. Some of these persons died in the first few days purely of radiation effect. The army assumed responsibility for the care of civilian as well as military casualties, although the two large army hospitals on the military reservation had been destroyed. Military hospital detachments were brought in from elsewhere. Accessory aid stations were established in certain buildings on the outskirts that had survived complete destruction, and in adjacent communities such as Oshiba. One of the most active in the city itself was at the Fukuramachi school. The Red Cross Hospital, despite severe damage to its fine building, took care of 1,000 persons as in-patients, and in addition conducted out-patient clinics. According to the director, Dr. Hachiya, the Post Office Hospital began to receive patients by 9:00 A.M. of August 7, and by the end of that day 400 had been given immediate care. A major installation was established on August 25 by the Tokyo Dai Ichi Military Hospital (the Walter Reed Hospital of Japan) at the living quarters of the Daiwa rayon mill at Ujina—later to be the base of operations of the Joint Commission.

The investigation of the effects of the atomic bomb was begun by the Japanese as early as the first day following the explosion, when Professor Nishina, a quantum physicist, came to Hiroshima. On August 14, Dr. Murachi * and Dr. Kimura came and stayed approxi-

---

* Dr. Koichi Murachi, a senior biophysicist of the Institute of Physical and Chemical Research of Tokyo, later became a valuable member of the Joint Commission, especially in the investigation of factors in protection from radiation. He died on March 31, 1964, of leukemia.

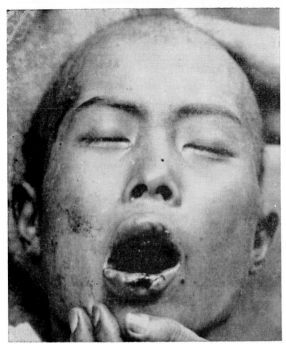

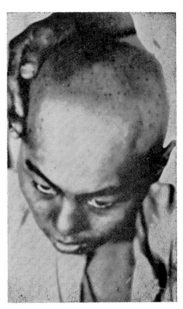

Left: A patient with dermatitis and epilation (First Military Hospital file). The distance from the hypocenter was not recorded, but it was probably within 1,000 meters. The patient was a soldier in the military compound.

Right: Epilation and petechiae in a patient exposed within the military compound at 1,000 meters. The patient (S——, H.-6176-U) died on August 31, 1945, when his white count had fallen to forty-five.

Left: Epilation which began on August 20 as seen on October 25, 1945, in a patient (M——) at the Ujina Hospital. He was a soldier who had been indoors on the second story of a two-story Japanese building at 600 to 700 meters. Slight downy regrowth of the hair has already begun.

Right: Epilation in a middle-aged woman, a patient at the Ujina out-patient clinic. Regrowth of the hair has begun in late October.

A street shortly after the explosion on August 6, 1945. The injured are seeking aid, probably in the shadow of Hijiyama. The city is burning in the background.

Temporary tentage, shelters at Hiroshima No. 2 Army Hospital, Moto-machi, August 9, 1945. An officer marches by at the left. (Nishina photograph.)

A nurse ministering to burned and injured patients, August 9, 1945. The scene is under tentage at the Hiroshima No. 2 Army Hospital at Moto-machi, staffed by the Second Provisional Fukuoka Army Hospital. (Nishina photograph.)

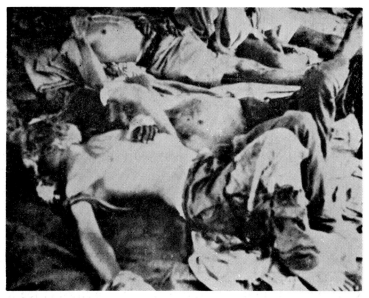

Burned and injured patients. (Nishina photograph.)

The Fukuramachi Aid Station, formerly a high school. (Bunka-Sha photograph.)

A clinic in session in early October 1945, before the arrival of the Joint Commission. (Bunka-Sha photograph.)

A bulletin regarding the whereabouts and condition of various persons, written on an interior wall at the Fukuramachi Aid Station. (Bunka-Sha photograph.)

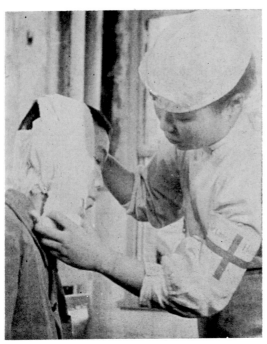

A nurse at the Red Cross Hospital administering treatment to a patient. (Bunka-Sha photograph.)

mately a week, and then returned later in the month accompanied by Dr. Miyazaki. With the help of the Neher cosmic ray counter they found a zone of gamma ray activity approximately ten times background in a region fifty yards across at the hypocenter. This was interpreted as the result of activation by neutrons of components on the ground. The radioactivity was far below hazardous levels. It is interesting to note that a part of this instrument had been made and tested before the war by Professor Neher himself in the United States. At Takasu to the south and west there was radioactivity of three times background level. It was interpreted as representing the effect of fallout directed by the wind that had blown from the east and by the rains that fell in this region just after the explosion. This activity was extremely low and certainly did not justify the fear of the rumor-mongers.

The physicists also noted the "shadows" cast on various objects as a result of the heat flash. By sighting along these shadows they were able to establish through a process of triangulation the position of the explosion. It is amusing that this datum, widely known among scientists in Japan in the second week of August, was considered a secret in the United States for many months.

Medical investigations were begun at once, and some of the earliest autopsies were performed at the Iwakuni Naval Hospital. At the Communications Department Hospital careful records of approximately 150 patients were kept and autopsies were performed by Professor Tamagawa of Okayama University in a makeshift autopsy room on the grounds of the institution. The Prefectural Hospital at Kusatsu was active until November 1945. Autopsies were performed there by Professor Araki of the Kyoto Prefectural University. Patients were transferred to military hospitals at Okayama and elsewhere, and to civilian institutions and hospitals as far away as Osaka and even Tokyo. In these settings investigative work and necropsies were also performed.

One of the most important investigative units was that maintained by the Tokyo Dai Ichi Military Hospital at Ujina, which was superbly staffed. It had been customary for many of the best young Japanese physicians from the major universities to be recruited into the military soon after receiving their medical degrees. Of this group, Majors Motohashi, Misono, and Hata later made valuable contributions to the work of the Joint Commission. In addition, they had collaborated with physicians of the Tokyo Imperial University, who had sent investigating groups into Hiroshima and had also received materials for study at the university in Tokyo. A report concerning 712 of these patients, completed by personnel of the Tokyo Dai Ichi Military Hospital, represents an important original document.

A major tragedy was suffered by the highly competent group of investigators headed by Professor Mashita of the Kyoto Imperial University. They took up residence at the Ono Army Hospital in the village of that name on the coast a few miles south of Hiroshima. During the great typhoon of September 17, a landslide roared down from the steep hills behind the hospital to the sea, crushing several buildings in its path and carrying to their deaths ten of the finest medical scientists in Japan, including the famous hematopathologist Professor Sugiyama.

Among some of these groups of investigators there existed a certain jealousy of what might be called intellectual property, and communications among them were not free. Such attitudes are not unique to Japan but tend to prevail among scientific communities throughout the world. With a few major exceptions, these teams considered particular aspects of the problems at hand. Under the difficult circumstances, the generally high quality of the studies performed is remarkable.

In retrospect, it seems strange that a well-staffed and well-equipped medical team had not been organized by the surgeon general of the U.S. Army for the specific function of performing an intensive investigation of biological effects of the atomic bomb. It was said that the surgeon general had not been informed of the planned employment of this weapon against the cities. Furthermore, General Kirk's personal relationships with General MacArthur were reported to be strained. We knew that he had, during his tour of the western Pacific in 1945, been refused permission to land in the Philippines. Rumor had it that years earlier, when Kirk was in command of a military hospital in the Philippines, he had declined to admit MacArthur as a patient because the latter was then serving in a civilian capacity.

The need for a thoroughgoing medical study was clearly perceived by Col. Ashley W. Oughterson, then serving as surgical consultant to General MacArthur. Since he knew of no preparations that had been made from Washington he conceived a plan of action while still on shipboard with GHQ on route to Japan. This was presented as a letter and immediately approved by Brig. Gen. Guy B. Denit, chief surgeon, GHQ, U.S. Armed Forces in the Pacific. Colonel Oughterson laid down the major directions that were actually pursued by the investigating team, and his memorandum to General Denit is therefore reproduced in full:

ON BOARD
SS GENERAL STURGIS

28 August 1945

MEMORANDUM

TO: Brigadier General Guy Denit
SUBJECT: Study of Casualty Producing Effects of Atomic Bombs.

1. A study of the effects of the two atomic bombs used in Japan is of vital importance to our country. This unique opportunity may not again be offered until another world war. Plans for recording all of the available data therefore should receive first priority. A study of the casualty producing effects of these bombs is a function of the Medical Department and this memorandum is prepared as a brief outline for such a study.

2. The need for study at the earliest date possible.

The casualty producing effects of these bombs should be studied at the earliest possible moment for the following reasons:

a. Much of the data must be obtained from the interrogation of the survivors and the sooner this is accomplished the more accurate will be the results.

b. Post-mortem examination of the dead may provide valuable information as to the cause of death. Three weeks or more will have elapsed and opportunity for post-mortem examination will be limited to late deaths among the survivors. It is hoped that some post-mortem examinations may have been done by the Japanese and that these records may be amplified by early interrogation of the Japanese pathologists.

c. Accurate case histories by interrogations of the injured may provide the most reliable data. These should also be correlated with the physical findings and the necessary laboratory examinations.

d. Residual radiation effects have been suggested as a possible source of danger and while this appears to be remote, such a possibility should be investigated at the earliest possible date.

3. The scope of the study.

The total number of casualties reported at Hiroshima is approximately 160,000 of whom 8,000 are dead. Even though due allowance is made for inaccuracies in these estimates the scope of the problem is such as to require the organization of teams with interpreters in order to complete an adequate study within a reasonable time limit. These teams should include pathologists and clinicians working under the direction of trained investigators.

4. The data which should be obtained.

It is recognized that any plan for the collection of data should be modified according to the circumstances. The following suggestions are intended to indicate the minimum rather than the maximum data required to properly evaluate the casualty producing effects of these bombs.

a. The location of all casualties living and dead should be determined in relation to the bomb and plotted on a contour map.

b. All living casualties should be identified by number for location on the map and an exact description of the case kept in a cross index file. Standard diagnostic nomenclature should be used. Such a procedure is necessary in order to determine the different casualty producing zones.

c. The position or protection of all casualties should be determined since this may be a determining factor in blast effects and burns. (Standing, sitting, prone, indoors, outdoors, in shelters, trenches or behind walls etc.)

d. Consideration should also be given to such factors as contour, temperature, wind and humidity in relation to casualties. It is unlikely that the latter factors will be of much influence but contour may be of considerable importance.

e. Evidence of blast effect should be searched for in both the pathology and in the clinical history. X-ray evidence of lung pathology may be helpful.

f. Burns should be carefully observed as to degree and character, part of the body involved, rate of healing, cause of death, etc.

g. All casualties should be recorded as to whether they were due to primary effects of the bomb or were secondary to burning buildings, flying debris or falling walls etc.

h. Evidence of residual radiation effects. While there is little indication that such injury will be found it should nevertheless receive serious consideration.

i. Complete post-mortem examination should be performed

on all injured in whom the cause of death is not clearly established.

j. It is hoped that the Japanese may have already organized an investigation of the casualties but this is unlikely under the circumstances. However much valuable data may be obtained from interrogation of Japanese doctors and pathologists. Also data valuable from a negative standpoint may be obtained from uninjured survivors who were within the danger zone.

5. It should be emphasized that since the effects of atomic bombs are unknown, the data should be collected by investigators who are alert to the possibility of death and injury due to as yet unknown causes.

6. It is recommended:

a. That in view of the importance of the data to be obtained and in view of the magnitude of the problem that a committee be appointed by the Chief Surgeon to survey the possibilities of obtaining data and to direct the collection of the data needed to properly evaluate the casualty producing effect of the atomic bombs.

b. That the various aspects of the investigation of the casualty producing effects of the atomic bomb be correlated through the Office of the Chief Surgeon.

A. W. OUGHTERSON
Colonel, Medical Corps

After the GHQ group landed in Japan on September 1, 1945, it was learned that various groups of Japanese scientists had already conducted medical investigations on the patients in Hiroshima and Nagasaki. Contact was established with the Japanese government on September 3, and thereafter reports were received and liaison maintained through the GHQ surgeon's office.

At about this time a group from the "Manhattan District," the organization that carried the responsibility for developing the atomic bomb, arrived in Japan. Its mission was to conduct a brief preliminary study of the effects for an immediate report to Washington. The major function was to determine whether there was residual radioactivity in order to safeguard our troops. This group, under the command of Brig. Gen. Thomas Farrell, was self-contained, with its own air transportation and equipment. In charge of the medical section was Col. Stafford L. Warren, whose civilian position was that of professor of radiology at the University of Rochester. He was well

The Oshiba Aid Station. A patient brought in by cart receives treatment. (Bunka-Sha photograph.)

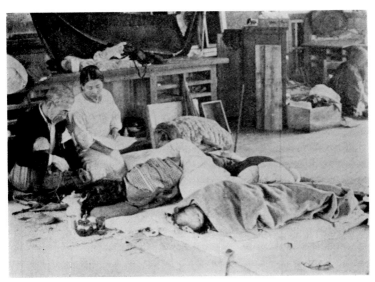

Families of patients assisting in their care. One of the two patients has suffered epilation. (Bunka-Sha photograph.)

The Communications Department Hospital seen from the rear (1,400 meters). The low building behind the central portion of the wall at the rear of the hospital was used as an autopsy room by Professor Tamagawa of Okayama University.

Professor Tamagawa in the autopsy room of the Communications Department Hospital at Hiroshima. (Bunka-Sha photograph.)

known to Dr. Oughterson from civilian life. On September 4, 1945, a conference was held with General Farrell and the senior medical officers, and it was agreed that it was desirable to unify the information to be obtained and to produce a joint medical report. General Farrell's group landed on Iwakuni Airfield, near Hiroshima, and made a preliminary survey of physical damage and of casualties in various hospitals and clinics. After the physicists had confirmed that only minimal radioactivity, well within the limits of safety, was present, the group returned to Tokyo some ten days later. Parenthetically, it is of interest that one localized but intense focus of radioactivity was found in the ashes of one of the crematories, but this was traced to a radium source that had been used for treating a uterine tumor.

It was obvious that for an intensive medical study the cooperation of the Japanese, who had already made all of the clinical and laboratory observations during the height of the early phase, was essential. Prof. Masao Tsuzuki, head of the Department of Surgery of the

Professor Tsuzuki's card.

Tokyo Imperial University and director of the Medical Division of the Japanese Research Council, was contacted. He agreed to enlist the full cooperation of Japanese medical scientists. As a result, the supreme commander directed the formation of a "Joint Commission for the Investigation of the Medical Effects of the Atomic Bomb in Japan." This was to include the Manhattan District group while it was still in Japan; a GHQ study group, still to be organized, which was to perform a more definitive medical study; and the Japanese government group under Professor Tsuzuki. Later, on September 25, there arrived a medical investigating team of U.S. Navy personnel (Nav Tech Jap, Team 11) under Comr. Shields Warren, M.C. This was composed of fifteen officers and enlisted men who were assigned to Nagasaki. With their arrival, it was obvious that duplication or conflict of effort would be ridiculous, and the Navy group then worked as part of the Joint Commission in full cooperation with the U.S. Army and Japanese components in Nagasaki. Dr. Oughterson proceeded at once to organize the GHQ group and to issue orders for designated personnel. It was on September 18, 1945, when the orders reached Saipan, that this daily record was begun.

CHAPTER 3

Preparations

Tuesday, September 18, 1945: At 8:05 on this steaming hot Tuesday morning received news verbally from the adjutant that I might be leaving "all over the Pacific." The somewhat garbled message had also stated that either Rosenbaum or Rosenberg was to be alerted to go along at once on the same expedition. Rumors were flying. We thought that most likely we would be sent to Japan—maybe to participate in medical work on the atomic bomb—but we hardly dared to think of it. Tension was high. Late in the morning a radio message was received by Jack Bumstead that confirmed our conjecture. Japan was to be the destination. It was Rosenbaum who was to go. Instructions were to take along two experienced laboratory technicians. Orders would be cut as soon as they were named. Picked Archambault and Reed, who seemed delighted. Called on C. G. and said, "Guess where I'm going." "To Japan, I suppose." "That's right." There was disappointment but also excitement in her voice. I immediately began to complete the few autopsy protocols and other remaining laboratory business and started to pack.

Orders for immediate departure arrived about 3:30 P.M. It was necessary to transfer all of the laboratory property to Captain Bornstein, who had been assigned as an additional pathologist some weeks before. He signed for $90,000 worth, with understandable reluctance. Hastily packed belongings were thrown into a station wagon. Quick and painful leavetakings were accomplished, but the arrival at the airport at 7:00 P.M. proved useless, since the last plane for Guam had left at 3:00 P.M. We had hoped to go on some unscheduled flight,

The next plane was due to depart at 8:30 the next morning. We returned to the Thirty-ninth General Hospital, leaving all of our belongings in the station wagon for early departure. At about 2:00 A.M. came a call from Major Tarnower on Guam, who had gotten confusing orders which were soon put aright since his name was unmistakably inscribed with mine on the orders.

[Jack D. Rosenbaum had come overseas with the Yale Unit, leaving his position as instructor in medicine. He was a brilliant student of Dr. John P. Peters, with a special interest in metabolism, and had served as officer in charge of the chemical laboratory. Arthur H. Rosenberg, who was in charge of serology, had worked at the U.S. Public Health Service Venereal Disease Research Laboratory on Staten Island. The original radio message was unclear as to who was to be assigned. Sgts. John Archambault and Jack Reed were both superb technicians and bears for work. Archambault had been a pharmacist in Fairfield, Connecticut, and Reed had been working toward an advanced degree in entomology at Rutgers. I was not sure that they would be happy with an extension of duty at a time when a return home was imminent. Confidence in these men proved more than justified, since both performed far beyond the call of duty throughout their tour in Japan.]

September 19: Arrived at airport at 8:00 A.M. and was told that all seats on the plane were taken. Our orders clearly indicated urgency, however, and places were therefore made available. Landed at 9:20 A.M. on Guam. Immediately made arrangements with the Naval Air Transport Service for departure to Japan on the first available flight, scheduled to leave at 10:00 P.M. that night. This left an entire day free. Contacted Dr. Harry Zimmerman, my former teacher in pathology at Yale, who was stationed with the Rockefeller Institute unit, which I had visited several weeks before, during the penicillin crisis. It was a well-spent day. Case records and cultures from our paratyphoid epidemic were turned over to Dr. J. T. Syverton. Saw Dr. Norman Stoll and demonstrated our *Isospora hominis* pictures, in which he had expressed an interest during my previous visit. After lunch went to the native hospital at Agana with Dr. (Commander) Sulzberger, who had become interested in cutaneous diphtheria after I had described our long experience with it, both in our troops and among the natives, during our previous visit. At the hospital we smeared and cultured what looked to me like diphtheritic ulcers in a number of natives. The demonstration of bacilli in the smears proved completely successful, much to Dr. Sulzberger's and Dr. Syverton's surprise. I then was brought to a meeting at the 204th General Hospital that was being conducted by the pathology service. Dr. Humphries very kindly took me under his wing. After the meeting and a good supper, was driven to the airport, where a C54 NATS aircraft No. 56494 was waiting for us. We reported to the desk at 9:00 P.M. and boarded the plane at 9:40. The take-off was exactly as scheduled at 10:00 P.M.

[The Rockefeller unit, under the command of Dr. (Captain) Thomas M. Rivers, M.C., U.S.N.R., served a research and consultative function, and was superbly staffed. Dr. Zimmerman had been an associate professor in the pathology department at Yale while I was in my residency. Dr. Norman Stoll was a parasitologist at the Rockefeller Institute at Princeton and Dr. Marion B. Sulzberger a renowned dermatologist from New York. A previous visit, made on August 23 and lasting for the next few days, was precipitated by a problem involving penicillin therapy. We became aware of the difficulty at once, more or less by accident. I had been doing a study with Dr. Max Taffel of the penetration of penicillin into spinal fluid in craniocerebral injury. One day we found that the apparent blood and spinal fluid levels had fallen to approximately one-eighth of what they had been before on the same schedule of treatment. At that time we thought that the streptococcus that had been carefully transported from our previous station in New Zealand as a standard for testing penicillin levels had gone awry, although we had kept standard cultures in storage. On investigation we found that a new batch of penicillin had been put into use in the hospital on the day the old material became outdated, as ordered. When we tested the outdated penicillin it was found to be fully potent, while the "fresh" batches were not. We therefore received permission at once from the island surgeon to use the outdated material, after it had been tested for potency. This local decision was against general policy, but it was surely wise, and it may have been lifesaving. At this time we also asked for transportation to the Rockefeller unit on Guam to test both our standard streptococcus and the various batches of penicillin.

Col. Verne R. Mason

Prof. Kanshi Sassa

Maj. Milton L. Kramer

Capt. Jack Davidson Rosenbaum

Col. George Veach LeRoy

Prof. Masashi Miyake

Sgt. Jack P. Reed

Sgt. John Archambault

Col. Elbert De Coursey

Comdr. Shields Warren

Maj. Samuel Berg

Maj. Herman Tarnower

The laboratory there quickly confirmed our results.

The paratyphoid epidemic which interested Dr. Syverton had occurred in an engineering unit on Saipan among sixty-five men, some of whom had shot one of the wild pigs on the island and barbecued it in a pit. Those who had eaten the pork on the first day remained well, but most of those who had eaten the unrefrigerated meat on the second day became ill, and two died. Many more undoubtedly would have succumbed had not all available physicians been mobilized at the 369th Station Hospital to care for the patients during the acute emergency. The problem was largely one of fluid replacement therapy. After the crucial first thirty-six hours the survivors began to recover, but they had a court-martial awaiting them on discharge, since eating native food had been strictly proscribed by the commanding general. Dr. Syverton had requested the cultures for study, and they were then delivered in person.]

September 20: The plane, although stripped for freight transport, had three central reclining seats with canvas backs, one of which I was invited to use. After a smooth flight we landed at Iwo Jima at 2:00 A.M. A three-quarter moon was shining, and the night was wonderfully warm and clear. We had a spectacular view of Mount Suribachi as we came in. The flattened top loomed over the end of the air field. The island is a dusty desert covered with rather heavy brown cinders. There are a few gnarled and twisted trees. The impression is quite like that of a disheveled Camp Stoneman. Orion, which we had not seen for almost three years, again clearly rides the sky near the horizon. We sought a middle-of-the-night snack and found it after much wandering about the airport. Then boarded the plane for another snatch of sleep and awoke on take-off at 6:30 A.M. The weather was wonderfully clear all the way up. Photographed Iwo receding into the distance, and also some of the Volcano Islands to the north.

[The weather on our trip to Tokyo had been perfection itself all the way. Yet we were to the south and east of a typhoon that was devastating Okinawa and lashing central Japan. This was to have some repercussions for our mission, since we learned later that color film which was sent to us had been damaged in that storm on Okinawa. Also, Hiroshima itself suffered severely. The city was flooded, and numerous landslides interrupted rail traffic. Most tragic of all was the landslide that killed the scientists from the University of Kyoto at the Ono Hospital.]

ITEM:
NIPPON TIMES
FRIDAY, SEPTEMBER 21, 1945
TYPHOON HITS FOOD CROPS

Kyushu, Shikoku Rice Affected Vegetable Farms Inundated

The typhoon which swept over the western part of Japan late Monday afternoon, caused considerable damage in Kyushu and Shikoku districts. After raging over Chugoku district and areas along the Japan Sea, the storm, said to be the most violent this year, was expected to pass over the northern districts and into the Pacific late Tuesday night.

Most hard hit were various districts in Kyushu and Shikoku where rice blossoms were just in bloom, and it is feared in these areas that this will have had effects on this year's rice crop. Inundations, it is also reported, caused damage to the growth of various vegetables.

Hitting Kagoshima in Kyushu about 2 P.M. Monday, the typhoon swept over the neighborhood of Hiroshima at 10 P.M. the same day and passed into the Japan Sea via the Sanin district. At 10 A.M. Tuesday, the typhoon landed in the vicinity of Niigata, previously crossing over Noto Peninsula, and then headed for the north.

In the Tokyo area a strong wind began to blow at dawn Tuesday with a velocity of 18.3 meters a second which at its height registered 29.8 meters and an atmospheric pressure of 743.7 millimeters. As a result, damage done was very slight. For a time the tramcar service in the suburbs was suspended but was restored to normal during Tuesday.

We had our first sight of the mainland of Japan at about 9:30 Tokyo time. There was an electric, almost crackling, thrill of excitement as we stood against the windows on the port side of the aircraft to regard and photograph the land that had so disordered our lives. We could see the white line of the breakers pounding a promontory and the dark hills beyond. Many of the villages were intact and looked peaceful enough nestling in the valleys with the terraced rice paddies rising above them, tier on tier. But many of the

Two views of the damage caused by a landslide at the Ono Hospital, near Hiroshima, which occurred shortly after 10 P.M. on September 17, 1945, during a typhoon. Here were lost ten scientists from Kyoto Imperial University, including Professors Mashita and Sugiyama. The survivors wrote: "With much regret, we, therefore, had to stop our work in Hiroshima and return with the ashes of our friends."

Iwo Jima: Mount Suribachi shortly after dawn, September 19, 1945.

Iwo Jima receding, on the way to Japan.

Landfall, Japan, 9:30 A.M., September 19, 1945.

Approaching Kiserazu Airfield.

U.S. ships of the line in Tokyo Bay, as seen from a TBM on the way to Yokosuka.

Approaching Yokosuka.

coastal towns were devastated and the shells of houses and often merely their outlines, were visible. Masses of rubble appeared to have been tidily piled to clear the roads. The countryside looked clean, green, and inviting. In harbors along the coast there were some land-based mock-ups of battle ships obviously designed to deceive. Our course took us over Yokohama. As we flew over Tokyo Bay we sighted ships of the U.S. fleet, flags flying. At 10:15 A.M. we touched down at Kiserazu Airfield. We had hoped to arrive at Atsugi but were told that MacArthur would permit only army planes to land there and that Kiserazu was the terminal for NATS. We were met by a young navy lieutenant who helped us with arrangements to call GHQ in Tokyo. The effort was entirely in vain. We knew that we were across the bay from Tokyo. The lieutenant told us that the distance by land was about ninety miles and that he had no motor transportation to get us there. We could get to Tokyo by train but the trains were still under Japanese control and were said to be crowded beyond capacity with the citizenry, whose animus toward us we could not judge. I had no stomach for taking this plunge, what with the interrupted sleep of the night before and the additional burden of our luggage. We then decided that we would make another attempt to call army headquarters later and busied ourselves with inspecting Kiserazu. Jack Rosenbaum said the place was aptly named. The field had been bombed and remnants of Japanese planes were still scattered about in disorder. Japanese gun emplacements and dugouts had been left exactly as they were. At water's edge we saw people peacefully gathering mussels from the foul-smelling water. On the field there were three white planes of the DC-3 type marked with green crosses. These were said to have flown the Japanese peace envoys. The interiors were well fitted-out with plush seats, but in complete disarray. Many printed and handwritten documents were scattered about in the aisles. I saved a few as souvenirs. Then returned to make another attempt to ring Tokyo—again without success. After some coffee and further talk with the sympathetic flight officer, he suggested that he could have us flown in TBM's to Yokosuka Airfield—on the great island naval base off Yokohama now under occupation by our navy and marines. This would at least bring us to the proper side of the bay and sixty miles closer to Tokyo. I had no clear idea of what a TBM was, but agreed with enthusiasm. These turned out to be single-engined torpedo bombers (Martin) which, while not designed for transport duty, do very well in a pinch. Luggage is put into the bomb bay. One passenger rides in the gunner's seat behind the pilot and the other in the second gunner's blister below. Two planes were assigned. Colonel LeRoy and I rode in the first and Major Tarnower and Sergeant Reed in the second. A party consisting of Captain Rosenbaum and Sergeant Archambault was left behind, to be delivered to Yokosuka as soon as one of the first planes returned.

The flight to Yokosuka occupied only a few minutes, and we were soon reunited in a huge hangar that was a madhouse of activity. At flight control, which was under the command of Marine Aviation, met Marine Major White, who said he didn't like the army but would nevertheless fly us to Tachikawa airfield in TBM's if we didn't mind riding pick-a-back. He said that although MacArthur had closed Atsugi to the navy, Tachikawa might still be open to "the enemy"—at least he had no orders to the contrary. We then quickly flung our luggage into the bomb bays with admonitions to the jovial pilots to keep them closed until we were at least over land. I rode behind the pilot in the gunner's seat and Captain Rosenbaum rode in the blister below. The view was magnificent. The ride was rather a thrill since our pilot suggested that we might like to see the Japanese fleet close-up on the way. He swooped low over the ships, many of which appeared to be dummies with wooden superstructure and mocked-up guns. Others looked to be of the first-line fleet but seemed largely deserted. We touched down at about 3:15 P.M. and the pilots hastily roared off to Yokohama before too many explanations of their possibly illegal presence could be demanded. Tachikawa was apparently a secondary airport. Many of the hangars had been blasted but others were still quite intact. Many of our C47 and C46 planes were all over the field.

Our efforts to telephone the chief surgeon at Tokyo again were completely unsuccessful, as the lines were still not in continuous working order. After explaining our mission we were very kindly assisted by Lieutenant Flook and Sergeant Bowen. They assigned us a station wagon and we were on our way to Tokyo, only twenty miles away. Tachikawa itself showed very little damage except for what we were told was the Mitsubishi airplane factory, which had been badly smashed. The countryside on the way to the capital itself was lush and beautiful. The road had long straight stretches with very few crossings.

Along the streets in the villages and even on the main road people can be seen dragging carts hugely piled with all sorts of goods and belongings including some apparently newly made boxes. Trade is obviously already beginning to revive. There are also many trucks with smoking, smelly, vertical wood burners mounted at the rear in substitution for the gasoline tank. Many are stalled, since, we are told, they require cooling, stoking, and cleaning at frequent intervals. Along the way are innumerable children who smile and give the V-for-victory sign. The grown women smile wanly; adult men are impassive but show no sign of hostility. As we entered the outskirts of Tokyo itself the horrible residues of fire and destruction were everywhere. Block after block had been flattened and only tall chimneys and a few concrete structures were standing. The streets had been cleared and rubble had been piled as neatly as possible out of the way of traffic. Only in the central portion of the city and the immediate vicinity of the emperor's palace was there a concentration of relatively intact buildings. One of the most imposing of these was the headquarters of the U.S. Armed Forces. It was a many-columned marble structure, formerly a life insurance center called the Dai Ichi Building. General MacArthur's five-star black limousine stood parked in front. Tall white-helmeted military police were on guard at the entrance. Shortly before 5:00 P.M. we met Col. Bruce Webster, surgeon, GHQ, advanced, on leave from Cornell, who said that he had been expecting us, seemed not too surprised at the difficulties of communication with Tachikawa, and was in every way cordial. At his suggestion we presented our orders at the NYK building. Our enlisted men were assigned to quarters in the Finance Building, a huge hollow square of massive gray stone, where they were registered at the headquarters of the Second Battalion First Cavalry Division. I was assigned a room at the Dai Ichi Hotel, roughly a mile from headquarters. This was a massive white-brick cubical structure with a tall chimney from which issued quantities of black smoke suggesting warmth and comfort. It stood in the midst of a devastated area stark against the elevated railway tracks and we noted that trains were running, all overflowing with people. I silently gave thanks that I had not chosen this method of entering Tokyo. Colonels and ranks to major were assigned to this hotel. I called Lieutenant Kaiser at the commandant's office and was able by special dispensation to obtain quarters with the rest of us for Captain Rosenbaum.

Elevators at the Dai Ichi were running perfectly and the atmosphere was that of a comfortable commercial hotel. The rooms were more than adequate, many supplied with private baths. Each had a very short and narrow bathtub lined by clean, small, rough yellow tiles. On each floor was an open office filled with affable but evidently poorly nourished young Japanese men eager to take laundry and perform all services. The first supper at the Dai Ichi could hardly be believed, after almost two years on Saipan. Food was actually served by charming Japanese ladies in colorful kimonos—the womenfolk of the men who would gladly have killed us little over a month before.

Just at the end of supper who should appear but Col. Scotty Oughterson in complete battle dress, looking healthy and happy to see us. He told us he had just come from Hiroshima and had seen that city as well as Nagasaki with members of the Manhattan District survey team that had been sent from Washington. They had made a preliminary survey of damage, residual radiation, and medical effects. Scotty's old friend Stafford Warren was with the group. He had been in charge of the medical department of the Manhattan District through the war. Warren's group would brief us at the earliest opportunity.

After dinner had a long talk with Scotty. Now for the first time we heard what our own mission was to be: the definitive study of the casualties, the collection of old data and materials, the determination of factors of distance and protection, and the preparation of a report on the medical effects of the atomic bomb. Both cities were to be investigated. I asked what help and equipment we would have. The reply was that we would be divided into two teams and that Col. Verne Mason would be senior medical officer at Hiroshima and Col. Elbert DeCoursey at Nagasaki. My assignment would be at Hiroshima, and George LeRoy would be with DeCoursey. We then decided that Rosenbaum would stay with me as he had throughout the war and that Tarnower would be with LeRoy. A few more American medical officers were on the way, but most of our associates would be Japanese investigators and physicians whose help Scotty had enlisted through the Japanese government. Dr. Tsuzuki would make the arrangements. He was professor of surgery at the Tokyo Imperial University and had been an admiral in the Medical Corps of the Japanese Navy. Scotty said that Dr. Tsuzuki was also a director of the medical division of the Japanese Research Council and had the best possible contacts throughout the country. In reply to my ques-

The Dai Ichi Hotel in Tokyo, September 1945. Welcoming smoke belches from the chimney. Although many of the surrounding buildings are rubble, this structure is intact.

A view from a room in the Dai Ichi Hotel, at dusk. On a clear evening the silhouette of Fujiyama, eighty miles away, can be clearly seen.

tion, Scotty said that despite the formalities of "purging" of former Japanese military personnel Dr. Tsuzuki was of such stature that he expected no difficulties.

As for equipment, the answer was simple—there just was none and we would have to get it ourselves from American hospitals and ships and on loan from the Japanese institutions. We were at once to make up a list of what would be needed for the study. Scotty then showed me a copy of his memorandum to General Denit, which outlined his plans as he first conceived them. Then to bed full of worries, but lulled by weariness and the sound of whistling trains, and for the first time in many years the rumble of a city.

[Col. Verne R. Mason had been one of the senior medical consultants in the Pacific theater. He was a graduate of Johns Hopkins who had practiced in Hollywood for many years and had had a number of famous movie stars and other Hollywood personalities among his patients. Col. Elbert DeCoursey, M.C., an outstanding pathologist later to become a major general and director of the Armed Forces Institute of Pathology, was the only regular officer to be assigned to the group. He had been laboratory consultant in the Pacific theater. I had met both men on Saipan in the early spring of 1945 and was greatly pleased at the opportunity of being associated with them.]

September 21: To the chief surgeon's office at the headquarters building early in the morning, where we met Captain Nolan of the Manhattan District, a tall and very affable young man who gave us some preliminary details concerning Hiroshima. Most interesting was the fact that now at Tokyo convalescing from an illness was a Major Motohashi, who knew the fate of troops who had been stationed at certain definite places in Hiroshima at the time of the explosion. Obviously he was a man with whom to become acquainted. According to Captain Nolan, the Americans had been using Geiger counters and other detection equipment and had found no significant residual radiation. Apparently almost all of the radioactive materials were blown high into the stratosphere and were replaced by air from the sides. However, it had rained twice after the catastrophe. Most of the patients who had been within 1,000 yards had died. Many had multiple petechial hemorrhages and injury to the bowel.

While in the surgeon's office, I was given a mimeographed report from one of the Japanese commissions that had been to Hiroshima to study the bomb effects. This report was entitled "Physiological Effects of Atomic Bombing of Hiroshima" and had been translated by G2 (Intelligence Service). The subscript described the report as "Full Translation of Handwritten Carbon-Copied 'Reports 1 and 2 by Squad Investigating Atomic Bombing of Hiroshima,' Issuing activity was not stated, dated 1-2 Sept. 1945." This report was a systematic account nine pages long of patients treated in the Ujina Branch Hospital, which had been opened on August 25, when 500 patients were received. It classified patients as those who had suffered burns and those who had not. The former, when in the zone of radiation injury, had a much worse prognosis than unburned patients. The latter had developed alopecia at the tenth day and then after August 20, fourteen days after the explosion, fever, hemorrhages, and diarrhea. Leukopenia was also documented. The clinical descriptions were by Major Motohashi. Surgical notes were by Professors Tsuzuki and Ishikawa. There was also a description of autopsied patients by Dr. M. Miyake, listed as assistant instructor in pathology at the Tokyo Imperial University. Among the treatments listed was autotransfusion of twenty parts of blood and two parts of citrate injected intramuscularly into the thigh. The report also contained a map showing the center of the explosion and the location of a number of the patients included in this study. The translation had been well done by laymen but contained a few bizarre sentences, such as, "The red corpuscles showed signs of multiple dyes," which, translated from English into medical terminology, I presumed to mean "polychromatophilia."

[Later information disclosed that this Japanese medical report was the first version of a very much longer report produced by personnel of the Tokyo First Military Hospital and the Tokyo Imperial University, which was issued much later. The final report combined not only these early observations, which were subsequently communicated to the American members of the Joint Commission, but also observations made during the operation of the Joint Commission in Hiroshima. This final report first was issued in mimeographed form and by several years after my return was undergoing deterioration. One copy was therefore laminated for preservation in the Yale Medical Library.]

Later that morning in the surgeon's office at headquarters met Professor Tsuzuki, the professor of surgery at the Tokyo Imperial University whom Scotty had mentioned previously. He was a tall, impressive, dignified gentleman, obviously a commanding presence. His use of English was perfect and it was soon revealed that he had studied oncology and radiation therapy at the University of Pennsylvania in the twenties. Dr. Tsuzuki was fully apprised of the purposes of our mission and was in complete sympathy with the necessity of performing a complete medical study. He stated that both superior medical personnel and skilled students would be supplied as teams to help in the work. The University of Kyushu, near Nagasaki, was to provide similar help to the group that was to be quartered there. I mentioned the need of equipment and materials. We agreed that a list must be made up at once and that we should meet the Japanese who would be working with us on the next morning to discuss what would be needed for the actual mission. Colonel Oughterson invited Professor Tsuzuki to supper with us that evening. In the meantime we were to make an expedition to tap American sources for as much of the necessary equipment and materials as we could obtain.

Spent the rest of the morning at work with George LeRoy and Jack Rosenbaum preparing an equipment list. In the early afternoon drove with Oughterson and LeRoy the thirty miles to Yokohama and the Eighth Army headquarters, where the office of the Eleventh Corps surgeon was located.

A broad highway connects Tokyo and Yokohama. It is still rough and pockmarked with poorly repaired bomb craters. Traffic is heavy and slow. Along the side are the inevitable hand-drawn carts. Many of the lumbering wood-burning Japanese vehicles weave in and out and frequently become stalled. There is much impatient military traffic, chiefly of heavy trucks. What must have been numerous houses and factories and banks have been thoroughly pulverized and there is now the stark plain from which rise the chimneys of houses and factories. Often these are intact, suggesting that fire rather than blast had destroyed the buildings. Most grotesque are rusted bank vaults still standing stolidly on heavy foundations. Yokohama itself has also suffered much, but some of the major buildings are still standing.

At the surgeon's office every help was promised us. However, we were informed that medical supplies were extremely scarce and that they were not due to arrive for quite a long time. We then talked with Major Partridge, to whom we supplied a complete list of the most important materials that were desired. He at once brought this over to the warehouse of the twenty-ninth Medical Depot Company for search. Then "home" to the Dai Ichi Hotel.

Professor Tsuzuki arrived promptly at 6:00 for supper, which was had, after a little whiskey, in Colonel Oughterson's room. Col. George LeRoy was there. At this time Scotty received various gifts, including a wonderful cypress wood Daruma statue. This represented a priest belonging to the sect of Zen, whose chief occupation was thinking. I thought the gift appropriate. The talk is largely on the cooperative nature of the venture and the types of studies to be undertaken. Doctor Tsuzuki said that there were still many patients in the hospitals representing the more serious cases of aplastic anemia from radiation injury and that these required detailed study. Japanese investigations were still proceeding. Many of these had been begun weeks previously. We would try to consolidate all of the information from these various groups as well as ourselves carry on a direct study of survivors, both in the hospitals and clinics. Dr. Tsuzuki promised to have prepared listings of all hospitals and investigating teams that had records and materials, and assured us that everything would be made available to us for a joint report. As for our own work, systematic records would have to be kept. We would need to design a standard record form which would include not only clinical and laboratory data but also information on factors in protection such as shielding, clothing, etc. We agreed that duplicate records would be kept and the forms prepared both in English and Japanese. Drs. Oughterson and Tsuzuki promised to design a record form and submit it to us and others of the group before it was finally duplicated. For record-keeping a map would also be needed, circled to indicate various distances from the hypocenter and also divided into sectors. These would assure that patients from all parts of the city were represented. A properly designed survey would indicate whether the effects were symmetrically distributed. Dr. Tsuzuki said he could find some good maps and Scotty thought that our map service could make the overprints and reproduce as many copies as were required. Dr. Tsuzuki said that the "Japanese young doctors" who were to work with us had already been selected and were on call. We agreed that we would meet with them at Tokyo University in the office of the dean of the Medical School tomorrow morning at 9:30.

Tokyo Imperial University in 1945.

The Institute of Pathology at Tokyo Imperial University.

The evening was a pleasant one, and I received the impression that we were dealing with a highly able and intelligent man of honor.

[This impression was abundantly confirmed in all of our relationships subsequently. Professor Tsuzuki was also a man of spirit and was quietly confident that his country would regain its status. One evening many weeks after we had arrived at Hiroshima, in a lecture on burns attended by some of the Americans and therefore given in English, he said: "Unfortunately my studies on burns were interrupted by the end of the war, but my son will carry them on." Twenty years later his son, Dr. Masakazu Tsuzuki, was indeed studying cardiovascular surgery at the Tokyo University under Prof. Seiji Kimoto.]

September 22, 1945: On this, a Saturday morning, we met for the first time the group of Japanese physicians and investigators who had

Left to right: Dr. Ishii, who was of the greatest help in the pathology studies in Japan, with his assistants Drs. Ebato and Shimamine. The latter performed much of the histological work in Hiroshima.

Members of the Joint Commission. Front row, left to right: Drs. Hatano, Murachi, and Nakao. Rear, left to right: Drs. Kato and Kakehi. The late Dr. Murachi was a brilliant biophysicist to whom is owed much of the credit for the work on the shielding studies.

been summoned by Professor Tsuzuki, the men who were to assist us in the atomic bomb investigation. I was amazed that they could be gathered within the brief span of time since our discussion of the previous evening. It left little doubt regarding his power and influence.

The scene in the large conference room at the university was unforgettable. At the large T-shaped table covered with a dark-green cloth were places for the senior Americans and Japanese. Against the back of the oak-paneled chamber, rigid and expressionless, almost immobile, there sat in rows of straight-backed chairs the flower of the younger medical talent in Japan. Tea was served. Introductions were formal, and somewhat strained. Few of the Japanese could speak English with the polished accuracy and fluency of Dr. Tsuzuki and some knew only a few words, but could communicate well with those of us who spoke German or French. Among the most impressive of the senior men was Professor Sassa, the head of one of the university medical departments, a man well-trained in physiology, who had worked in London with Starling, and Dean Tamiya of the Medical School, a bacteriologist. Impressive also were Dr. Yoshikawa, a chemist, and Professor Miyake, who had just been made professor of pathology, a towering, graceful man with a grave, aristocratic manner, whose second language was French.

Colonel Oughterson made a little speech in which he emphasized that the war was over, and that in any event science was nonpolitical. He said that physicians and investigators had a loyalty to science, and that the needs of mankind would be well served by a thorough and informed study of radiation effects; that the study could obviously not be performed by us without help, not only because of the language barrier but because we needed the highly skilled medical scientists for which Japan was famous. Finally, he stressed that the work would be truly a joint effort, that we would expect the full cooperation of the Japanese in obtaining complete information, but that it would never be our intent to rob them of the fruits of their thought and work in publication. Dr. Tsuzuki translated these remarks as they were made. He then replied in like spirit in English and Japanese and gave assurance that the best men would be available, that they would work and help unstintingly, and that they would withhold nothing—in accordance with the expressed wishes of the emperor. He also expressed the hope that this effort would be a first step in restoring to normalcy scientific relationships between our nations.

GENERAL HEADQUARTERS
UNITED STATES ARMY FORCES, PACIFIC 119
AGPD-A

Advance Echelon
APO 500
22 Sep 1945

AG 210.453 AGPD

SUBJECT: Order.

TO   : Off & EM concerned, orgns indicated.

      Fol-named off & EM now on DS Advance Ech, this hq, **MP**
Hiroshima, Nagasaki and such other places adjacent thereto as
may be necessary on TDY for the purpose of carrying out
instructions. Off & EM are auth tvl between Hiroshima and
Nagasaki at such times as may be necessary in the accomplishment of their mission. Upon compl will ret this sta. Tvl by
mil acft is dir for accomplishment of an emerg war mission.
Govt mtr and water transportation auth. Personal baggage not
to exceed 50 pounds auth each off & EM while traveling by air.
Provisions of par 26, AR 35-4820, 19 Apr 45 apply. Per diem
auth each EM while traveling by acft in accordance with Sec I,
AR 35-4810, 19 Apr 45. Use of Govt qrs and messing facilities
enroute by EM is mandatory. 65-***** P432-02 A 212/60425.

LT COL AVERILL A. LIEBOW	0463559 MC	39th Gen Hospital, APO 244
LT COL GEORGE V. LeROY	0418636 MC	374th Gen Hospital, APO 105
MAJOR HERMAN TARNOWER	0482553 MC	304th Gen Hospital, APO 247
CAPT JACK D. ROSENBAUM	0403070 MC	39th Gen Hospital, APO 244
T Sgt John P. Reed	31098996	39th Gen Hospital, APO 244
Tec 3 John J. Archambault	31105220	30th Gen Hospital, APO 244

By command of General MacARTHUR:

R. W. BOLLING
Major, A.G.D.
Asst Adjutant General

DISTRIBUTION
  Off & EM concerned (5 ea)
  Chief Surgeon, Adv Ech (1)
  CO 39th Gen Hospital, APO 244 (1)
  CO 304th Gen Hospital, APO 1058 (1)
  Fiscal Off, AFWESPAC, APO 707 (1)
  Dir MR Div, AGO (1)
  Dir Contl Br (2)
  AG GHQ (8)
  AG Rear Ech (1)
  AG-Records (7)
  AG-PE (1)
  Hq Comdt, Adv Ech (1)

Orders to carry out the mission at Hiroshima and Nagasaki.

As we later mingled with our colleagues-to-be they seemed very intelligent, alert, active, and eager to begin. If there were fears and reservations, they were not difficult to understand and were in any event well-hidden by the quiet formality and reserve of the meeting.

We then went to the Pathology Department, which had a large building of its own. Here cups of Japanese tea were again served. This was, although unsweetened, sweetish with medicinal overtones, of a pale yellow-green color, altogether warming and cheering. It definitely helped to introduce and smooth conversation. At this time the plans for dividing available young men into Hiroshima and Nagasaki groups for the pathological aspects of the study were discussed and a tentative arrangement was arrived at. We discussed what equipment would be needed. Professor Miyake also told us of what pathological materials had already been brought to Tokyo and said that he would give full cooperation in their further study.

Immediately after luncheon Colonel LeRoy and I made another arduous trip on the crowded road through the devastated landscape to Yokohama, where we found, much to our dismay, that almost none of the equipment or materials that we had requested through Major Partridge were available, except for some nonspecialized bulk items in classes seven and nine. We made a list of these for requisitioning by Colonel Webster. Then, by accident, we heard that an abandoned Japanese laboratory was housed in the very building where Lieutenant General Eichelberger had his headquarters, and that there was another one several houses away on the same street. We went at once to the building and found a remarkable picture of wanton destruction. The laboratory had apparently been used for analyzing fish meal and similar materials and contained large quantities of bottled chemicals. Many of the labels were in Japanese and unintelligible to us. An abundance of glassware was present, which was of enormous help to our spirits. Then home after an extremely rough ride over the crater-pocked roads. Stopped in Colonel Webster's office and obtained from him a requisition for the items in stock at the Twenty-ninth Depot.

In the evening had a hot bath, a good supper, and then made a search for Sergeants Reed and Archambault. However, neither was to be found. I left a note for them informing them of progress. The walk back across the long dark alleys was ghostly with the skeletal hulks of buildings lining darkened streets and hundreds of burned-out cars lying about in confusion.

Found Colonel Oughterson and told him of our discouragement in locating equipment. I showed him the long list of things that we required which were listed as nonavailable at the medical supply depot. There were only a few glimmers of hope because, according to Major Partridge, materials were daily coming off the ships at Yokohama. LeRoy and I were planning to return there tomorrow and would check further on this point. Scotty admitted that he was surprised that medical material was in such short supply, although, after all, we had been in the country in force for not more than two weeks. He had already inquired about equipment at the Forty-second General Hospital, which had opened a short time ago in Tokyo. They could spare nothing and were able only to beg a few items themselves from the hospital ship *Marigold* which was in the area. He would obtain a list of other hospitals and their locations from the Surgeon's office and would send various members of our group to forage. He said also that we could always be sent what we needed after we got down to our laboratories and that hospitals would undoubtedly be opening up in southern Honshu near us. My reply was that it would be much better to have everything on hand so that we could start work at once on what would probably be a dwindling patient population.

One bright spot after a disheartening day was the arrival of Colonels DeCoursey and Mason, who were bubbling with enthusiasm. They said that they had been worried about us since several military planes had been lost in the typhoon of September 17–19. We assured them that we had been in the clear smiling sunshine to the south and east. DeCoursey was reassuring about our supply troubles, saying that he knew that plenty of everything was on the way.

September 23: Set out again for Yokohama bright and early by truck with George LeRoy. We first went to the warehouse with our official requisition to obtain the supplies that were said to be in stock. These included: 50 gallons of DDT; 10 hand sprayers; 48 Freon aerosol insecticide bombs; 24 mosquito bed nets; 10,000 multivitamin capsules; a mass of housekeeping supplies such as soap, Brillo, etc.

[We had every intention of keeping well while in Japan. We had no clear idea of the circumstances under which we might be living and therefore determined to come well prepared. We were concerned about Japanese type B encephalitis, but actually found mosquitoes

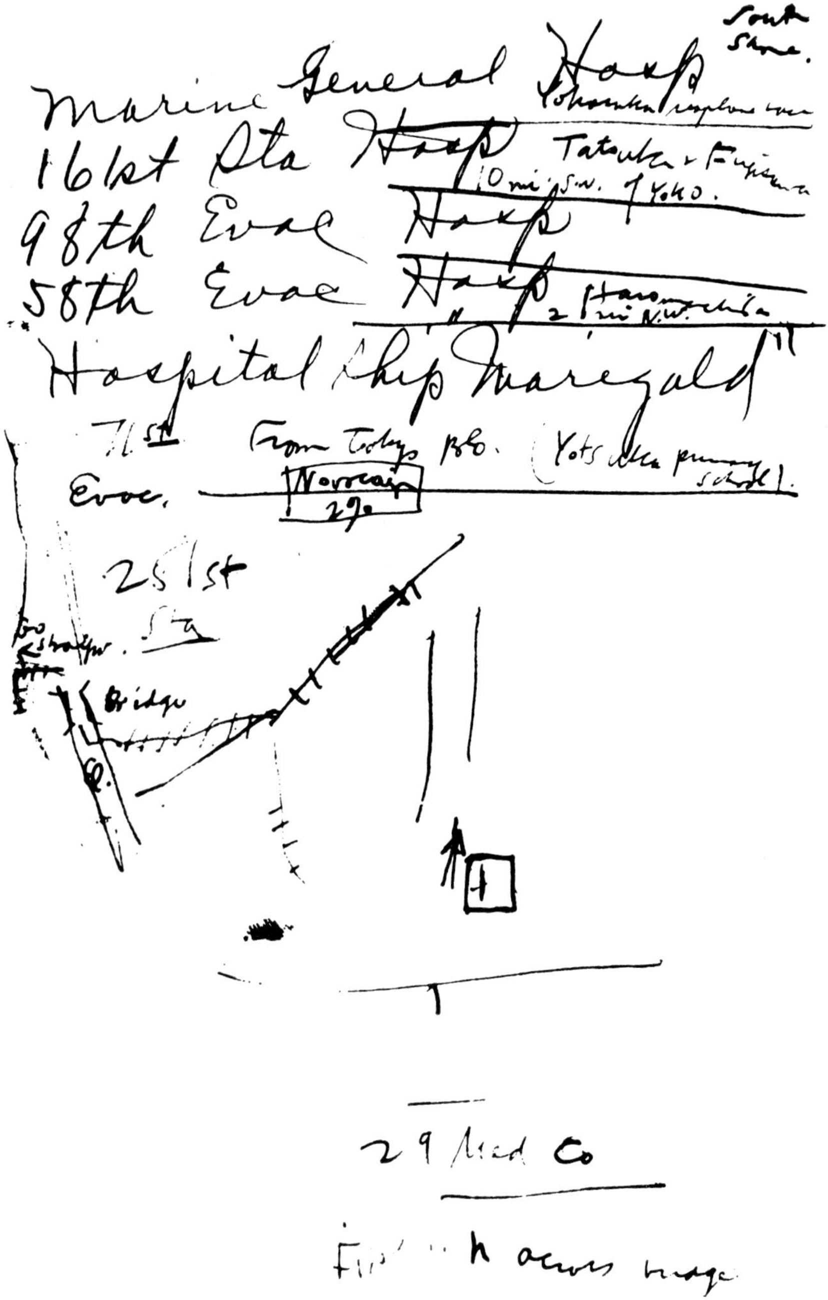

Marine General Hosp [South Shore.]

161st Sta Hosp

98th Evac Hosp

58th Evac Hosp

Hospital Ship "Marigold"

71st Evac. From Tokyo 180. (Yotsuka primary school)
Norecair 29

251st Sta

Bridge

29 Med Co

Scribblings listing possible sources of materiel, with directions.

as well as flies to be scarce by the time we arrived in Hiroshima. The multivitamin pills were to be used as "treatment" for patients in the clinics, since we had been advised by our Japanese colleagues that custom required the physician to give every patient some type of treatment after examining him. Actually the fee is considered payment for the treatment, not for the diagnosis. The vitamin pills were good-looking, would be entirely acceptable to the patients, and could certainly do them no harm. We found, however, that they caused us one problem since some patients thought they were endowed with magical properties and therefore came to the clinics more than once, thereby introducing a slight bias into our survey procedures.]

Then, on the advice of Major Partridge, to the warehouse of the 268th Quartermaster Battalion, which was located after a little difficulty. No officers in authority were present. Crates of supplies were continually arriving by truck from the docks. We found a tractable sergeant who was directing the work. We told him of our mission and of our desperate need. He said that most of the crates contained mixed goods and that the only way to tell what was in them was to read the manifests. Most of the material destined for the hospital consisted of sponges, urinals, and the like. Some of the crates, however, among other things, contained some laboratory supplies. Those that we designated were cheerfully opened on the spot and the required materials identified and laid aside. The procedure was somewhat irregular, but everything was considered expendable and our sergeant seemed not to have a worry in the world as long as we signed for what we took. We told the sergeant to keep a sharp eye out for microscopes, centrifuges, and other major items, and said we would be back in a few days. We were graciously invited to lunch at the warehouse—a lunch which consisted of a large square of well-prepared luncheon meat in a blanket of scrambled eggs. This was a much tastier meal than the Spam that had been our lot in many of our island experiences previously.

Then off to raid the laboratory that we had inspected on the previous day, after obtaining a large quantity of packing material from the quartermaster. Things were then rapidly loaded onto a truck with the aid of our very cooperative driver. A wonderful spirit of helpfulness was displayed by all with whom we came in contact, and there was practically no red tape. A disturbing experience was the hunt for a balance that we had noted on the preceding day in the headquarters building. After a thorough search, it was discovered in another room, where it had been moved since the preceding day. We considered ours to be the prior claim, and in the absence of dissension made off with it. Then a long, cold, and bumpy ride back to Tokyo and on to the university, which we found after much difficulty in the dark. Here, in the Pathology Department, we dumped all of the material that we had acquired. There was considerable excitement at our haul. The Japanese were especially interested in the DDT and the aerosol cans.

After a hot bath, an additional warming was had over some Canadian Club, and everybody was in high fettle. Later there was a meeting in Colonel Oughterson's room—all hands present including Captain Nolan. There was much wind and little turning of the mill was accomplished until we got down to the serious business of discussing details of the record forms which Dr. Oughterson had roughed out. His considerable experience with abbreviated records in the Connecticut Tumor Registry, of which he was one of the founders, had stood us in good stead. It was well designed and occupied only two sides of a single sheet. Names were to be recorded in both Japanese and English. All locations were to be by zone number of the maps that had been designated and were in preparation. Some ambiguities were clarified after argument. We agreed finally that in the short form certain rules of thumb would have to be followed; for example, dates of onset and cessation of signs and symptoms would have to be inserted wherever possible. The form stressed radiation injury and factors in protection. We realized that there might be some difficulty in distinguishing flash burns from flame burns. Presumably Dr. Tsuzuki's group was making a similar critique. Scotty also reported that the maps were to be ready in a day or two and presented us with the list that we needed of hospitals in the area. We agreed with enthusiasm to make excursions to them in search of additional supplies. Since I was planning another trip to Yokohama in a few days, I picked the Marine General Hospital at the Yokosuka naval base and the 161st Station Hospital.

[When these records were designed, we did not sufficiently realize the difficulties of identifying persons by their recorded names in Japanese. Since alternatives are available, transcription is especially

Check List

1. Name   Age   Sex   Occupation or rank
2. Location when injured (locate by zone map number): *If < 1 km.: not injured*
3. Primary Injury by,   Bomb;   Burn   Blast   Radiation
4. Secondary Injury by: Burning Building   Flying Debris   Falling Walls etc.
5. Protection   *Direction of Blast?*

   a. Position: Standing   Sitting   Prone
   b. Indoors: Concrete Building *which*   Brick Building   Japanese Building
      Covered earth or concrete shelter
   c. Outdoors: "In open" Behind wall   In trench   Behind tree, post etc. *Be sure meaning is understood.*
   d. Clothing *1. Standard Terms. 2. Flame char scorch Unchanged* — *SPECS*
   e. Any other protection: *Buildings, etc.*
6. Were others present?   Were they injured?
7. Burns: Degree - 1st   2nd   3rd   Area, percent   Part
        Healing   Eye injury
8. Radiation Effects:

Symptoms	Time Onset	Time Ceased
Nausea		
Vomiting		
Cramps		
Diarrhea		Watery Bloody
Malaise		
Anorexia		
Gingivitis		Necrotic
Pharyngitis		
Purpura Petechiae Epistaxis	Other Hemorrhage	
Epilation *Examine personally*	Scalp Eyebrow Beard Axillary Pubic	

SPECS

Skin pigmentation: *And Dirt*   Red   Dark Brown   *Describe on reverse side.* *Depigmentation*

Absence of sweating: Head   Chest   Genitalia *Erection!*

Complete History   Menstruation   Abortions   Potency *Coitus Pollution Libido*

Where indicated make special mention of shielding from gamma rays:

9. Blast Effects:

	Early	Late
Lung		
Ears		
Intestine		
C.N.S.	*Headache?*	
	Unconsciousness?	

- 1 -

The front face of the record form used by the Joint Commission. Written in are the original notes used as the basis for discussion with the Japanese members.

GENSHI BAKUDAN SAIGAI CHŌSA JIKŌ

District of [illegible] Hospital

JUSHIN TSUKIHI	JUSHINSHO	CHŌSA-I
SEIMEI	UMARE NO GAPPI	SEI SHUKUGYŌ MATA WA KAIKYŪ
JŪSHO(ATENA)		NAIGŪSHA KODOMO

CHIZU NI YORU TAIBANGO

1. BAKUGEKI TŌJI NO IDOKORO

2. SAIGAIIN: ICHIJISEI; PAKUSHA, NESSHA, HŌSHA.
      NIJISEI; KASHŌ, GAISHŌ.

3. BŌRIJŌTAI

   a. SHISEI: TACHI, SUWARI, FUSE, FAGAMI.

   b. MUKI: MAE, USHIRO, MANANE(MAE MIGI, MAEHIDARI, USHIRO MIGI, USHIRO HIDARI)

   c. OKUNAI: (NANKAI DATE NO NANKAI) KONKURITO   RENGA   MOKUZŌ   CHOKUSHA
      MATA WA KAGE.

   d. OKUGAI: KAIHŌ, MATA WA KAGE.

   e. BAKUFU WO SAEGIRU MONO(KONKURITO, MOKUZŌ, RENGA SO NO TA.)

   f. BŌKUGO; CHIJŌ MATA CHIKA, ŌI, TSUCHI, KONKURITO, KI)

   g. KIMONO(SHURUI, MAISU, IRO)

   h. SONOTA SHAHEI(BŌSHI, TETSU KABUTO, TEBUKURO)

4. KINPEN TANIN NO UMU   SONO HIGAI

5. NESSHŌ:TEIDO   FUKASA   KUI   FSIKA.

6. ME   NIMI

7. GAISHŌ,SHURUI TEIDO   VEIVA

8. TOJI NO KENKŌ JŌTAI, BYŌKI   SO NO HEIHA
   OMONA KIGŌRŌ(TOGFI OYOFI PYŌRI)

9. SONO GO NO KODŌ:YUKUSHICHI, KINITSU   TSUTOME OYOFI SEIKATSU.

10. SHŌJŌ: a. ISHIKISHŌJI   b. MYALI

       c. ZUTSŪ   d. HAFIKE

       e. ŌTO   f. HARAITAMI

       g. GERI   h. KEIREN

       i. SONOTA SHOKISHŌJŌ

       j. SHOKUSHI   k. ZYŌZAI

       l. SHUKKETSU
          PIKA, BUI   TEIDO(TAISŌ)   SURUI(IRI, HANA, DAI)
          KAGUKI, HANAJI, TETSUNETSU, MAE ETSU, TOFETSU, KETSUREN, KETSUNYO, SONOTA.

       m. KŌMAEN SHIGININ, EMGETSU.

The Japanese record form used by the Joint Commission.

difficult. We erred also in not recording the original home address of the persons as an additional means of identification. As the records were being analyzed, some misunderstandings came to light with respect to "epilation," since in some instances no distinction was made between epilation resulting from radiation effect and that resulting from burns. This in large part was more due to the difficulty of the examining physician in communicating with the patients than it was a fault in the design of the records. Similar problems were encountered with reference to hemorrhages, since some of these were traumatic or associated with disease unrelated to radiation. Human frailties involved in filling out questionnaires and records were revealed when we discovered some 35 instances of what were thought to be duplications in over 6,000 cases. The congruence of recorded facts, even as to dress, was far from perfect. Yet in general, most of the major facts, although recorded by different observers, seemed to have been accurately stated, and furnished a basis for confidence.]

It was already considerably into the next day when the meeting broke up. In my room, I opened an "acipak," the soldiers' comforter, and found some cigarettes, fine for small gifts and tipping, some hard chocolate, which was the object of my hungry search, and some shaving equipment.

September 24: On the way out to the University, went in search of our sergeants, since we wanted their help in packing our plunder. Found them and learned that they had been visiting the Nikko shrine some ninety miles away! They were among the first Americans to be there since the war. During the morning, major decisions on the disposition of the Japanese physicians were made. Drs. Tsuzuki and Nakao and our senior people considered the list of the twenty-five whom we had met several days before in terms of specialties so that we would have a reasonably good distribution of talent for the two cities. On the advice of the Japanese, who thought the load of work would be greater in Hiroshima and said that Nagasaki had a well-established group of Japanese physicians at the Navy Hospital, fourteen were tentatively assigned to Hiroshima and eleven to Nagasaki. I marked the names of those assigned to Hiroshima with an *H* on my list. Dr. Nakao also wanted to be part of the Hiroshima group since he had been studying a collection of bone-marrow slides and peripheral

1. Dr. Yoshikawa — Biochemistry
2. Dr. Suwa — Pathology
3. Dr. Ishii H — Pathology
4. Dr. Ohashi — Pharmacology
5. Dr. Hakamada — Psychiatry
6. Dr. Murathi H — Radiobiology
7. Dr. Kubo, H — Internal Medicine, Spirochaetosis
8. Dr. Kitamoto H — Internal Medicine, Tuberculosis
9. Dr. Tsukada H — Internal Medicine, Clinical Chemistry
10. Dr. Hashimoto — Internal Medicine, Gastrology
11. Dr. Weda — Internal Medicine, Cardiology
12. Dr. Nikaido, — Internal Medicine, Physical Therapy
13. Dr. Yamamura — Surgery, Penicillin
14. Dr. Ishikawa H — Surgery, Fracture
15. Dr. Urabe — Surgery, Tuberculosis
16. Dr. Kajitani H — Surgery, Cancer
17. Dr. Hatano H — Surgery, Neuro-surgery
18. Dr. Ooto, — Orthopedic Surgery
19. Dr. Ogoshi H — Urology, Andrology
20. Dr. Yasuda H — Dermatology
21. Dr. Ito H — Gynaecology, obstetrics
22. Dr. Kawamura H — Pediatrics
23. Dr. Kashiwado — Oto-rhino-laryngology
24. Dr. Kabshi — Radiotherapy
25. Dr. Yamakawa H — Internal Medicine, Cardiology.

Dr. Nak...

The first list of "Japanese young doctors" supplied to the Joint Commission. Those designated by an *H* were assigned to Hiroshima. A few changes were made later.

blood collected from patients there by the team from the Tokyo First Military Hospital and Medical School and the Tokyo Imperial University. The Hiroshima group also was to include Dr. Murachi, a biophysicist who had done some of the earliest measurements of residual radiation and other physical effects.

[Dr. Kiku Nakao was a charming young assistant professor in Dr. Sassa's clinic who proved to be a brilliant hematologist. He made numerous major contributions to the work and to our happy collaboration during our stay in Japan. After the war he held an investigatorship at the Argonne National Laboratory in Chicago and spent a pleasant few days with us in New Haven. Later he became professor of medicine at the Tokyo National University.]

The remainder of the morning was spent in identifying materials that were still needed for our work with our Japanese colleagues. They were quite willing to designate centrifuges, ovens, staining jars and other glassware, chemical solutions, and stains from the various laboratories of the university. Also suggested that each unit take along some of the useful reference books. These were gathered together from various personal libraries. Many are pirated U.S. texts reproduced photographically. There were both volumes of Peters and Van Slyke. Made a mental note to bring a pirated edition back to Jack Peters. Especially admired is the German hematology by Rohr. This will be an interesting companion to my Wintrobe which I had carried in my luggage from Saipan. These were gathered together and the remainder of the morning was spent in packing, using the materials that we had brought up from Yokohama.

Home for lunch and then returned to the university in the afternoon to continue the work. For the first time found time to go on a shopping tour. We had passed what looked like a print shop on our trips to the university. I went on foot and found some striking prints in the Sakai shop. There were some fine old prints on rice paper among dozens that were available. Selected some amusing Utamaros and others.

Late in the evening Scotty appeared and announced that he had arranged for airplane transportation for equipment and personnel, including the Japanese. An estimate of the weight of the materials was to be made and the personnel were to be specified. The necessary number of planes would be assigned as soon as we had the information. We are apparently fortunate that the air force has very little to do at this juncture with its huge number of men and ships, and they promise to cooperate fully with us.

September 25: Walked to the surgeon's office after breakfast but found no further crystallization of plans. Was delighted to find that the maps were ready. The Hiroshima map was Japanese and had all of the important features marked both in Japanese and in the Latin alphabet. The circles around the hypocenter were made at intervals corresponding to 500 meters for the first 3,000 and at 1,000 for two

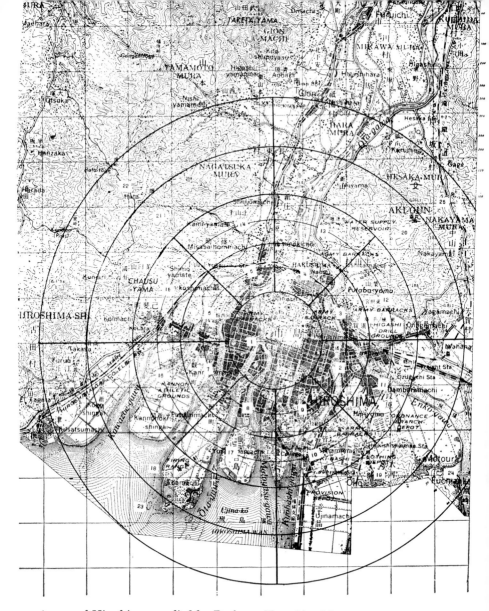

A map of Hiroshima supplied by Professor Tsuzuki, with an overprint by
the U.S. Army Map Service designating ring zones and sectors. This map
was used by the Joint Commission for survey work. The darker rings
are drawn at 1,000-meter intervals around the hypocenter. The military
encampment is the pale area within the innermost ring.

more rings beyond. These were intercepted by radii drawn from the hypocenter. In this way twenty-five zones were delineated. Thousands of the record forms had also been mimeographed and were brought with the maps to the university, where the packing was being completed. Since the preceding afternoon and during the morning various little prizes were brought in by members of the team who had visited the various hospitals. These, together with the Japanese contribution, gave us the rudiments of two laboratories and equipped us also for a little clinical work. Practically all of the major items of laboratory equipment were from the Tokyo University. Packing of what was there was completed toward the end of the morning. Spirits had clearly risen when the work was done.

After lunch again took the opportunity of exploring Tokyo on foot with Jack Rosenbaum. The city was very crowded and our soldiers were everywhere. Walked much of the length of the Ginza in the central district. Although there had been bomb damage, many of the buildings seemed intact and some were already under repair. Some of the rubble in the central district was being cleared by our engineers with bulldozers and other heavy equipment. Great crowds were standing by, gazing in amazement at monsters such as they had never seen. Our men seemed to be enjoying being the center of attention and gave some virtuoso performances. Shops along the Ginza were filled with all sorts of goods. We found the Mikimoto jewelry store was groaning with beautiful artificial pearls. The most interesting sight, however, were the carts which lined the curbs. These were full of all sorts of interesting mass-produced cheap trinkets such as cigarette lighters, but also produce and a few handcrafted things. Bookstores were full of recently printed magazines, pamphlets, and books. They were crowded and the crowds included some curious G.I.'s browsing. The better stores are particularly jammed with soldiers and Japanese mingled in friendly confusion. We found a large department store, comparable to our best, Takashimaya, where I bought a lovely painted silk screen and lacquer plate.

On returning to the Dai Ichi was told that a navy commander had flown a seaplane to Hiroshima. He landed in the harbor, which was hazardous since it was still mined, but was able to taxi in and explore the city. He reported that there was extensive damage from the typhoon of September 17–18 and that the airfield was flooded, making landing there impossible for some time. Also, rail traffic was blocked by landslides. On this discouraging note went to bed.

September 26: Called first at the surgeon's office to see about developments but found nothing exciting. There met Lieut. Col. James French, a pathologist from Dr. Weller's department at Ann Arbor. He had been given the assignment of making a survey of Japanese laboratories and had done considerable traveling about the country. He joined me in the drive to Yokohama in the truck which I had ordered in order to continue the next stage of the foraging expedition, and particularly to check on our good sergeant and any equipment that he might have sequestered for us. On the way down, French told me about some priests who had been in Hiroshima and who were in the Catholic Hospital in Tokyo. Their condition was said to be poor. Thought it would be interesting to visit them if time allowed, and obtained directions to the hospital from French. I noted that a strong centrifugal movement of our troops appeared to be taking place from Yokohama and that even the Quartermaster Depot was about to be moved. No really useful laboratory items had turned up in the new consignments. I did, however, pick up 45 cases of Ten-in-One rations and thirteen cases of K field rations. This was authorized by Major Prentice on the basis of "thirty men for twenty days." We would at least have a good food supply to start with. Also, to my pleasure, found winter field clothing available and bought a new pair of field shoes and a fine Eisenhower jacket, which I had not seen before in the Pacific. Drove on to the Marine General Hospital at the Yokosuka base but came away empty-handed, despite a pleasant reception. The 161st Station Hospital, however, was able to spare syringes and needles, and, to my surprise, an autopsy kit.

On the way back in the open cab of the truck I was rather chilled, and in the afternoon took a much-needed nap. Was awakened in midafternoon by Colonel Oughterson, who said that the Nagasaki group was to leave tomorrow. I was charged with the responsibility of attending to the loading to take place at the University in the morning. Was also informed that during Professor Tsuzuki's absence, Professor Sassa would be the chief liaison officer with the Japanese group and that Dr. Nakao, of his department, would be his aide.

September 27: At a very early hour went directly to the university. The trucks lumbered up shortly thereafter. The equipment which had been designated for Nagasaki was checked off as it was loaded into the trucks. Innumerable Japanese physicians and younger students, together with their anxious families, were milling about. To add to the difficulty, Sergeant Archambault, who was to go to the airport with the Japanese and to continue on to Nagasaki, was not to be found for some time. Finally he arrived. In his efforts to check out he had been delayed in what he called a "bread line" in the Finance Building and could not get away. All of the personnel was finally gotten aboard the trucks with firm instructions from the senior members of their party not to move until the roll was called. This was finally achieved and the caravan was safely off.

Checked in at headquarters and received nothing but discouraging words on prospects for getting the Hiroshima section off and away. Then returned to the university to find Dr. Ishii, the pathologist scheduled to go with us to Hiroshima. He appeared tired, sad-faced, and unshaven, and was dressed in the remnants of a thin military uniform and sandals. We discussed in halting German and English further plans for the pathology study. Conversation was especially difficult because of the Japanese custom of replying affirmatively to all questions even though the sense of the answer is intended to be negative, for example "Yes, it is not so." He told me, to my great pleasure, that he had some protocols and materials already in hand. I replied that I would look forward to reviewing the materials with him and to translating the protocols. I expressed especially my desire to have a competently staffed and equipped histology laboratory so that we could cut and stain any old blocks, and prepare the new cases as they became available at Hiroshima. After a difficult and lengthy discussion, I was not quite certain that I had been fully understood, and I was especially disturbed by the fact that he never smiled, nor did he have the affability of most of his colleagues.

[The reason for Dr. Ishii's apparent reluctance to become friendly with Americans became evident during the next few days, when I gingerly inquired of others about his apparent depression. The best answer came much later from himself, in a letter that he wrote in December after we had completed the work in Hiroshima and returned to Tokyo.

Despite his personal tragedy, Dr. Ishii gradually became a firm friend, and my later experiences with him in traveling and working together remain among the most cherished memories of my assignment in Japan.]

Dear Mr. Liebow.

I am very sorry to say,but there is one matter I want to
ask you.
I have lost my posts, as you know,Institute of Jap.Cancer
Reserch was burnt,St.Lukes Hospital,where I was working as
a director of laboratory,is now used by Allied Force,so I
can get incomes from nowhere. I am now looking for my job
as a doctor everyday,but its rather difficult to find it soon.
My father and my wife of my bosom were died at the bigining
of this year and my two young children are left behind,so
I must support them. Unfortunately I have suffered from
bombdamage two times,all my havings were burnt out and now
I am confronted by crisis of everydayliving under such a
terrible inflation nowadays.
Is there any way to find suitable workplace such as Occupation-
armyhospital,or if not,usual office?
I am indifferent about the sort of works, but I hope job of
laboratorywork at hospital as technician or translation.
Would you call at every likely place,if you please,though
my vocabulary is very poor,and I am afraid I could not be
employed?
I want 500 or 600 Yen monthly if possible.

Yours Sincerely

Z. Ishii

The letter from Dr. Zenichiro Ishii which explained his situation. It
was delivered on December 15, 1945, after he returned to Tokyo from
his service with the Joint Commission at Hiroshima.

Later, in conversation with Dr. Nakao in the hematology laboratory, there was much more rapport, and a preliminary review of well-stained and well-interpreted hematology slides was presented. This was the first contact with actual material from patients at Hiroshima and I found it most exciting. The marrows, mostly obtained from patients three to four weeks after the bombing, showed essentially the findings of aplastic anemia. We discussed the interpretation of certain cells and agreed that they were atypical derivatives of reticuloendothelial cells resembling plasma cells and that the designation "plasmacytoid" was appropriate. Dr. Nakao promised to organize this material and to make the clinical records available. This would keep us well occupied and would also represent an actual start on the work of transcription onto the Joint Commission forms that were now ready.

In the early afternoon back to the hotel. Was asked to translate a remarkable document at the request of Col. Stafford Warren. This was an eyewitness account of the explosion and of the city and people in the days immediately following, written in German by a Father Siemes, a Jesuit priest who had been living in the hills of Nagatsuka, some three miles from Hiroshima. It told in detail of the rescue of four of his brethren who had been injured in the city during the explosion. I read the story spellbound and horrified. By late afternoon most of the translating had been done. It was dictated to a remarkably skillful sergeant of General Farrell's Manhattan District Group who typed the translation directly as it was spoken.

[This stirring, beautifully and modestly written description records Father Siemes' impressions as he witnessed the tragedy from his room at the Novitiate of the Society of Jesus. This group of Jesuits had been evacuated to Nagatsuka from Tokyo some six months previously. It is a detailed account of the flight of survivors from the city and of the involvement of the priests, one of whom had studied medicine, in the work of rescue. Father Superior LaSalle and three other brothers had been in the central mission and parish house in the city at the moment of the explosion. They were brought to Asano Park along with many others. Two of the brothers had only minor injuries but were completely exhausted. One of these was Father Kleinsorge, who had been mentioned by Colonel French, and whom I met later in Tokyo. Father Kleinsorge was not able to walk and was left behind to be brought out on the following day. The priests ministered to many other people and brought fifty of them to the monastery for care. As Father Siemes put it: "Our work was, in the eyes of the people, a greater boost for Christianity than all our efforts during the preceding long years." One of the most fascinating aspects of this account is the philosophical consideration of all warfare, and specifically of the use of this weapon: "It seems logical to us that he who supports total war in principle cannot complain of a war against civilians." Remarkable also is his statement of the attitude of the people: "None of us in those days heard a single outburst against the Americans on the part of the Japanese, nor was there any evidence of a vengeful spirit. The Japanese suffered this terrible blow as part of the fortunes of war—something to be borne without complaint."

Father Siemes' account became a major source of material for John Hersey's masterful *Hiroshima*, and it was published in full, in my impromptu translation, in *The Saturday Review* several years later. The translation, I fear, did less than full justice to the style, excitement, and literary merit of the original German.]

A delightful talk and drink before supper in the chambers of Colonel Oughterson. In the late evening took occasion to write letters home and to C. G. and to read descriptions of the intricacies of the Japanese drama: Noh, Kabuki, etc. Then tired, but happy, to bed.

September 28, 1945: First thing in the morning we were greeted by new arrivals, including Philip Loge, formerly a Yale medical student whom I had taught. He is eager to transfer into the Hiroshima group, and this is finally arranged. Maj. Milton Kramer of New York has also been assigned, as has a laboratory man, Maj. Samuel Berg, a worried bachelor much concerned about who is to take responsibility, especially in working with the Japanese. He rushes about trying to obtain additional supplies, but by the end of the day his success unfortunately is minimal. Capt. Calvin Koch, a pleasant, keen-looking youngster, joins us later. These are our long-awaited reinforcements.

Later in the morning also met Capt. Paul O. Hageman, a former colleague on the house staff at the New Haven Hospital, and Lieut. Col. Hymer Friedell, from Western Reserve University and the Manhattan Project. Colonel Friedell gave us a lecture on radiation phenomena. This dealt with elementary principles and definitions. This was a well-presented and useful review for all hands, since none of us could qualify as an expert in radiation biology. Of particular importance was his implication that radiation injury in these cities could be considered essentially a gamma ray effect, like that of hard X-rays. There may have been minor exceptions. Neutrons traveled far enough to reach the ground, but only in a small area beneath the explosion. Induced radioactivity was therefore not a major hazard. The same seemed to be true for fallout, insofar as the investigations were carried. Specific information, if known, was considered classified.

Later in the morning went to see Dr. Nakao again, and he indeed proved to be in possession of a veritable gold mine, consisting of peripheral blood and marrow smears of no less than forty-four cases that were worked up in Hiroshima from late in August to September 15. Among these were fifteen fatalities, of whom seven were autopsied. Agreed with Nakao to begin the work-up of these with him tomorrow.

After lunch found General Farrell's expert stenographer and finished dictating the translation of Father Siemes' account to him. I was now all the more anxious to find the German Jesuit priests at the International Catholic Hospital. Captain Rosenbaum is eager to come along, and we make first for the St. Luke's Medical Center, which is said to be not far from the Catholic Hospital. On the way we pass the astonishing sight of a huge mosque, intact and glittering, complete with dome and minarets. St. Luke's is an impressive modern skyscraper situated in an only moderately damaged residential zone. It is now designated as the Forty-second General Hospital. We were met by Major Vollmer, who provided a brief tour.

There is a beautiful chapel. The laboratory is already functioning. During the war it was used by the Japanese, who were reluctant to return it. It escaped significant damage, but under the press of war it went into a physical decline from which it is now being rehabilitated. General MacArthur has favored this place. It is currently in the charge of Colonel Yeager. A Philippine banner has been presented to the hospital, together with a portrait of the general by Mrs. MacArthur.

Obtain more precise directions to the Catholic Hospital at St. Luke's, and we make our way through a largely burned-out portion of the city. Finally we find the hospital with the aid of two small Japanese boys. The hospital itself is intact and spotless. We meet

Mother Harse, a most gracious Englishwoman, who is in charge. After tea we are ushered in to meet Father Kleinsorge. This is our first direct contact with an actual patient. We have a long conversation in German, which he obviously likes to speak, although his English is also quite good. He tells in his own words of his experiences, so graphically described in Father Siemes' account. He is amazed at our knowledge of the story until I tell him of the translation of the Siemes document, and then he has a good laugh. He is a keen, kindly man, thin and pale but showing remarkably few other effects, except that his wounds have failed to heal, now some seven weeks after injury. Partial healing had begun, but at three weeks the wounds began to suppurate. He developed a leukopenia. Then home through the dusk after a fascinating day.

SEIBO BYOIN
INTERNATIONAL
CATHOLIC HOSPITAL
Tōkyō Yodobashiku, Shimoochiai,
2 *chōme* 670.

國 際 聖 母 病 院
東京淀橋區下落合二丁目六七〇

The letterhead of the hospital where Father Kleinsorge was a patient.

September 29, 1945: Colonel Mason and I were joined by Lieutenant Loge and Captain Koch on a visit to the University. There Nakao met us and the first part of the work of reviewing the records began. These appeared to be excellent, except that many of the actual marrow counts have not as yet been done. We therefore subdivided ourselves, Japanese and Americans, into teams of counters and record translators. There was a master summarizing chart. Colonel Mason busied himself with a transcription. The chart obviously was the result of a great deal of extremely painstaking effort. After lunch we returned, also bringing Major Kramer, and continued the work. Then a long walk home.

The Jesuit Monastery at Nagatsuka, from which Father Siemes witnessed the atomic bombing of Hiroshima.

St. Luke's Hospital in Tokyo, used as the Forty-second General Hospital by the U.S. Army Occupation Forces.

The Tokyo First (Dai Ichi) Military Hospital, the Walter Reed Hospital of Japan. The Japanese Army Medical School was also located here.

In the evening met Maj. Sylvan Moolten. He is assigned to the surgeon's staff. He has had extensive experience in pathology gained at Mount Sinai Hospital in New York, although he is primarily a clinician. He is a very keen and thoroughly delightful man who discusses knowledgeably many of the things we have seen in the Pacific, including cutaneous diphtheria.

September 30, 1945: At breakfast on this pleasant Sunday found that Colonel Mason was leaving for the Nikko shrine. Decided to spend the morning closeted in my chambers reading and writing letters home, to C. G. and to Paul MacLean.

In the afternoon, took the opportunity to explore the city with Jack Rosenbaum and Milton Kramer. Jack had told me that he had seen people actually starving or ill to the point of unconsciousness at the railroad station. Although the economic state of the country was at a low ebb and rationing was strict, I found this difficult to believe. But there were indeed frail, dull-eyed people begging, and some, even children, lying huddled with their parents—a pitiful sight. Passersby seemed to pay them little heed.

We went by Japanese taxi, a smoker driven by an intrepid man who must have been trained on a juggernaut, to Ueno Park, a famous beauty spot. This was crowded on the brisk afternoon with strollers and both Japanese and American soldiers. One of the loveliest sights was a five-tiered pagoda with its graceful roof and its glowing red-ocher sides. In the city below the park, things were quite as busy as on the weekday. We were amazed at the immense crowds filling Ueno railroad station and overflowing to the outside. There was no pushing, and everything was patience and courtesy. Bemused, we walked the long distance back through the darkening but bustling streets.

October 1, 1945: To work again early in the morning. Counted innumerable cells, but in the hypoplastic marrows these are widely scattered and often difficult to classify, and the work is progressing slowly. Dr. Nakao is most helpful, most sincere, and clearly expert in hematology. Captain Koch and Lieutenant Loge devote themselves mostly to the peripheral bloods.

Consulted with Colonel Friedell regarding the possibility of some of the Manhattan District team coming to Hiroshima with us, but his group has decided to continue back to the U.S. Later met Colonel Mason, who had returned from Nikko that noon. Although our expedition is now poised, we must await the return of Colonel Oughterson from Nagasaki before making final arrangements.

Today acquired information concerning two new recruits. Our request for clerical assistance was met by the assignment of Staff Sgt. Hial D. Huffaker and Pvt. Michas Ohnstad, from the Twelfth Cavalry and First Cavalry Artillery respectively, who are to go with us. God grant they can type!

October 2, 1945: Worked all day at the university with Colonel Mason and all of the junior officers and our Japanese colleagues. Got well in sight of the end of the blood counting.

Then I had another difficult working session with Dr. Ishii. Despite our language problems, it is quite clear that he is a very well-educated pathologist. He showed me some twenty-six necropsy protocols. These seemed very well worked up and illustrated with sketches. Although the bulk of the description is in Japanese, many of the technical words are in German or Latin. Weights of organs are in Arabic numerals. There are many sketches. It is possible to understand in reasonable detail the substance of the description. This we test by going over one or two protocols. For the first time I see Dr. Ishii smile as some comical misinterpretation on my part is made. It was agreed that eighteen of these cases would be cut here in Tokyo and that the rest would be brought along with us and cut after we arrived in Hiroshima. We could then complete the microscopic descriptions for this prime group in direct personal contact while carrying on our other work. Dr. Ishii will also bring along a large number of marrow contact preparations that come from the autopsy material. Actual preserved organs of the same patients from whom we have blocks in Dr. Ishii's group are said to be in "enlarged pieces" in Hiroshima at the Ujina Hospital. Among other important information obtained this afternoon is that Major Yamashina in the Japanese Army Medical School has some well-preserved material from the very earliest cases. Most of those in Dr. Ishii's possession are from a group who succumbed from three to five weeks after the bombing. We take note that Major Yamashina must by all means be found.

We decide also to bring with us to Hiroshima Mr. Shimamine, a medical student, who is said to be an expert in cutting sections. He

The pagoda in Ueno Park.

The Ueno railroad station. Immense crowds patiently await transportation.

is a charming, slight, gently smiling young man of studious appearance who comes from one of the families important in the professorial ranks of the Tokyo Imperial University.

While waiting for a seat at the supper table, met up with Captain Nolan and Col. Stafford Warren. The latter was an elongated, spare, gray-haired, mustached figure, looking the picture of a pukka sahib, but with a mild and gracious manner. He expressed his pleasure at the Siemes translation. Scotty, who had also returned from Nagasaki, was very happy to see us and pleased with the work that we had got in hand. In the evening had a long conference with Colonels Mason and Oughterson, and was told that Drs. Tsuzuki and Sassa and four of the younger Japanese, including Drs. Kitamoto and Okoshi, could get off to Hiroshima by plane on the following morning.

We hear now that the Nagasaki group is in excellent quarters at the Omura Japanese Naval Hospital and has no less than 150 cases of radiation sickness.

October 3, 1945: In the early morning Dr. Tsuzuki brought to the front of the Dai Ichi Hotel Dr. Sassa and the "Japanese young doctors." Finally, shortly after 8:00 A.M., all are ready to board the trucks to Tachikawa Airfield. The present plan is to have a shuttle plane in readiness for the work of taking all of us down. In the morning in consultation with the Japanese at the university prepared a list of the doctors in order of preparedness to go down. Among those ready is Dr. Kato, a debonair bachelor, who is to assist the men at Hiroshima in getting the early records of the forty-four cases up to snuff.

In the afternoon went to pick up the rations for the Hiroshima group. We found the Red Gate open. These cases were then placed into the hands of the Japanese at the Medical School, who seemed reluctant to accept the responsibility. We assured them that they would not be prosecuted by our M.P.'s. I found Dr. Ishii, who said that Dr. Tsuzuki was angry with me for not having discussed the Shimamine matter "through channels"! He had not mentioned his displeasure to me that morning, however.

After supper was informed that the plane bearing Dr. Tsuzuki and his companions had been forced to turn back from Hiroshima by heavy overcast and that on the way back its radio communications had broken down. The pilot had to fly the unpressurized airplane at over 14,000 feet to be sure to clear Fujiyama, which he could not see. Near Tokyo he found a hole in the clouds and was able to buzz Atsugi at dark. Flight control guessed that something was wrong. Cars and trucks were lined up to illuminate the airstrip. He landed safely after seven hours of continuous hazardous flying without any certainty of where he was.

In the evening, met none other than Col. Joseph Sadusk, who had arrived at the head of a typhus commission. There had been some outbreaks of what was considered to be true typhus fever in Japan, and some of our soldiers had come down with the disease.

[Colonel Sadusk had taken his residency in medicine at New Haven with Dr. Francis Blake and had started with the Yale Unit as a captain, but had been reassigned. He had done much distinguished work in epidemiology in Hawaii and with the U.S. Typhus Commission and was ultimately promoted to full colonel and decorated with the Legion of Merit. After a post-war career as an outstanding practitioner in Oakland, California, and then as a professor of community medicine at George Washington University, he became chief food and drug administrator.]

About 9:10 P.M., while I was playing cribbage with Major Kramer, Colonel Oughterson came and said that we were in fact ready to leave in the morning. This meant that we had to get ourselves and the enlisted men packed. Sergeant Reed was put in charge of the latter detail. In the meantime I begged a ride to the NYK building, to which Captain Rosenbaum had just been moved, and gave the junior officers the good news. Then a hasty job of packing my own belongings and to bed at 12:30 A.M.

October 4, 1945: Arose at 5:15, and after picking up Koch, Rosenbaum, and Loge rushed to the university. Then rapid loading of all our equipment and men with the help of numerous willing Japanese who got the whole job done in time to return to the hotel by 6:55. Breakfast had been arranged and we left the hotel at 7:30 A.M. Col. Mason claimed to know the way to the airport and seemed to be doing reasonably well at first. It was pouring—a real cloudburst. Finally, however, we became more and more lost and then the good colonel ultimately admitted complete failure. Then we struck out more-or-less cross-country, with the help of our inquiring Japanese companions, passing through towns such as Koraida and Yozakawa, but at long last made the correct turn and entered Tachikawa. Although we were very late, we were welcomed by our pleasant acquaintance Lieutenant Flook. Colonel Oughterson's party also had been late but was there when we arrived. I found a pilot talking excitedly with Colonel Oughterson. He had flown the Tsuzuki party to Hiroshima and was exhausted by the harrowing experience. Dr. Tsuzuki himself was at the airport looking none the worse for it and ready to take off again. We were at first rather hopeful of taking off, but at last the flight was declared closed. Disgustedly we struck out for home and found that the rain had in fact worsened. Deep

Aaf
4 oct 45 —

PASSENGER LIST FOR HIROSHIMA
=============================

Col Mason
Lt Col Liebow
Maj Kramer
Capt Rosenbaum
Capt Koch
Sgt Reed
S/Sgt Huffaker
Cpl Ohanstadt
Lt. Loge
Tec 4 Buckles
Dr Tsuzuki
Dr Kitamoto
Dr Tsukada
Dr Okoshi
Dr Nakao
Dr Motobashi (*Maj.*)
Dr Sassa
Dr Murachi
Dr Kubo
Dr Yamakawa   *Aheaf.*
Dr Ishikawa
Dr Kajitani
Dr Hatano
Dr Toii

15 Dr Gotoh
16 Dr Ito
17 Dr Kawamura
18 Dr Yasuda
19 Dr Kabohi
20 Dr Kato
21 Dr Shimazing
Lt O'Brien, Charles
Lt Goring
Ensign Reynolds, G. F.
Techn Smith
Techn Green
Techn Miller
Techn Brownall
Techn Block
Techn Sewa
Techn Sato, John (Interpreter)
Photographer Kasner

42 passangers

The list of passengers for the flight to Hiroshima, October 4, 1945, which had to be abandoned.

puddles were everywhere and many vehicles had become stalled in large lakes. Then back to the hotel to a fine dinner of Spam and cold cuts in the hot and sultry room.

In the afternoon slept the sleep of the extremely weary. Later in the evening again met Colonel Sadusk and we had a long talk about the good old days at Yale and our various wartime experiences. Bedtime was delayed by another conference with Colonel Oughterson. Col. Stafford Warren came in. He somberly showed us the destruction and radioactivity maps of the Hiroshima and Nagasaki areas. We also discussed the delayed effects of radiation on the bone marrow in the patients. He stated that these effects occur after relatively low doses. Colonel Warren said that Yawata had originally been scheduled for the atomic bombing but that the plans had been changed because of meteorological conditions. Then, finally and wearily to bed with a bad prognosis for tomorrow's weather ringing in my ears.

October 5, 1945: Heavy rains continue and no air transportation can be authorized. In mid-morning, a visit from Dr. Tsuzuki, who has apparently done much smoothing of the way for our work in Hiroshima. He says that the people are in fear of our troops and that this may inhibit our mission greatly. Dr. Tsuzuki then agreed to introduce me to General Hirai, who is chief of the Pathological Institute of the Japanese Army Medical School. This was accomplished after a long trip through the downpour. The general is a small man with a cast in his left eye and a friendly manner. The insignia on his collar resembles that of a U.S. Navy commander except that there is a small red star in the lower front corner of the collar. The promise is given to us that the slides of the earliest cases in possession of the Army Medical School will be delivered to us, together with the remaining tissues, by two medical students who will follow us to Hiroshima in about two weeks.

On returning, the question of food supply for the Japanese component of the investigative group is discussed at length by Dr. Tsuzuki and our group, and we agree that all of the doctors and possibly the students as well will be fed by us. Scotty emphasizes that this will have to be cleared by headquarters, since at this time it is forbidden to distribute American food supplies to civilians in Japan.

October 6–11: These days were spent in disgust at the downpour and wind, but there were some bright spots, particularly October 6, when I had the privilege of signing for six jeeps for our unit on transfer from General Farrell's group which was returning to the continental U.S. Now we had our own private means of getting about. There was also the pleasure of working at the university with Drs. Nakao and Ishii and exploring Tokyo on foot, wrapped in a raincoat. The population was still drably and poorly dressed, the men often in remnants of military uniforms or thin dark suits. Women were wearing the baggy trousers (*mompé*) that had been wartime wear by imperial decree. It was amusing to see the little Japanese police in dark blue, carrying small swords and directing traffic side by side with the strapping M.P.'s of the First Cavalry Division. The latter, who seemed to have been selected for their size, also stood guard at parade rest before the various gates of the palace and at the doors of radio Tokyo—station JOAK—whence had come the Tokyo Rose broadcast that we had enjoyed in the islands during the war. The Kabuki players reopened on October 3 in their own theater, and their popularity among the Japanese was attested to by the difficulty of getting tickets and by the plentiful speculators. Jack Rosenbaum was able to get tickets, and we enjoyed a dazzlingly colorful stylized performance and the symbolism of the action from reading, and kindly English-speaking Japanese were eager to explain the nuances. The audience was almost entirely Japanese. The performances are long, and it is customary to bring food.

Parts of many days and evenings were also spent in planning our approach to the work at Hiroshima. The shielding and protection studies would be most difficult. Scotty emphasized the need for a mortality and morbidity curve in relation to distance. We hoped that we could identify certain buildings and shelters at known distances from the hypocenter that were occupied by people whose precise positions at the moment of the detonation were on record and whose fate was known. Drs. Tsuzuki and Murachi said this was definitely possible and that in fact they already had a number of these buildings in mind. It was evident that if we considered only gamma radiation, as seemed reasonable, we could assume straight-line travel of the rays which would intercept the buildings at angles determined by their distance from the hypocenter. If we could then establish the structure of the buildings from building plans, the thickness of steel, concrete, etc., through which the radiation would have to penetrate to produce a certain effect or to be completely absorbed with no biological effect could be calculated. One could assume that the LD-50 dose (i.e. the dose that would be fatal to half of those exposed) would be in the range of 500 roentgens if delivered to the body as a whole. This datum could then give us at least a rough idea of radiation dosage under various conditions. There would be some error in the calculation from scattering of radiation. We also hoped ultimately to learn from the physicists who had designed the bomb both the spectrum and intensity of the radiation at the source. This, insofar as it was known, was still considered secret, according to Stafford Warren, who would provide no information except that there was a mixture of hard and soft gamma radiations. The hard rays have a shorter wave length and penetrate more deeply than the soft. Effects on tissues, however, would depend on the quantity of radiation absorbed.

In the meantime three C-46 aircraft that had been assigned to transport us were lying idle, and our patience was severely under test.

CHAPTER 4

The Encounter

October 12: Finally the dawn is beautifully clear. Consequently, called Tachikawa Airfield at 6:15 A.M. and was advised that the trip would be cleared for take-off. Called the "Japanese young doctors." On arrival at the university found that they were not at the appointed place at the Institute of Pathology. I was horrified for a moment but soon thought to look for them in front of the main medical building. There they were—all except Dr. Ishii. He had gone into the country again. Shimamine was there, however, dressed in his dark-blue student's uniform and wrinkled cap. Then off we went. Everything went smoothly this time except that the manifests had somehow become lost in the shuffle. However, after a little cajoling of the pilots we quickly prepared a new passenger list. They, for one thing, seemed pleased that we were at the rendezvous on time. This time Dr. Tsuzuki was not on the list as he had been on October 4, and there were no personnel who were not of our group. The three C-46's were loaded one by one and the heavy laboratory equipment and jeeps strapped to the metal floors; passengers were to ride in bucket seats at the side. Finally we got X-392 loaded and it took off. Similarly the second plane, X-372, was loaded, the passengers boarded, and a smooth take-off accomplished. All of the Japanese who were present had been assigned to these two airplanes, and I thought at first they had been loaded aboard. Shortly afterward I went back to attend to plane number X-131, which had not yet been loaded. A manifest was prepared and the load was put aboard, jeeps and all. Just as I was about to get the crew together there was a sudden loud tearing sound followed by an explosion. A large, shining, silvery C-47 on take-off had suddenly veered to the right and gone off the main runway, which was at a somewhat higher level than the parking field. It skidded into the rear ends of a number of parked planes which were in a neat row, tails to the strip on the field below. As it came crashing off the runway, it turned completely around and came to rest facing in the direction in which it had started. Its left wing had been shorn off and it was burning fiercely where it had torn at the fuselage. The pilot's compartment in front of the wing had fallen forward and was lying on the field in front of the body of the plane. A soldier, his uniform and hair aflame, came running madly toward us as we dashed onto the field. We quickly made for the plane on the windward side as the fire trucks came screaming up and quickly extinguished the fire. We first attempted to take care of the two boys who had been pinned in the pilot's compartment and were strapped into their seats against the instrument panel. They were obviously dead although seemingly uninjured. I gave first aid to a third boy who had been rescued from the body of the plane. I splinted another badly fractured left foot and arm with boards and strips of cloth and bandages that had been brought from the warehouse in an ambulance. There was no hospital near the field nor were physicians other than ourselves immediately available. Others were similarly handled. As I was splinting the arm of one boy whose elbow had been fractured, and who was among the less severely injured I looked up to see an air surgeon lieutenant colonel leaning over me. I said, "Thank God you're here," and he replied, "You're doing fine, Averill. I know even less orthopedics than you do." It was Dr. Thomas Warthin, who had been on the resident staff of the New Haven Hospital with me some ten years previously. He had finally arrived with supplies from the Air Force Hospital some miles away. We finished with the others and sent them all to his hospital. All had been taken safely out of the planes except one boy, who had been burned to death, and the pilot and co-pilot, who had been killed in the forward compartment.

We then cleaned up, and as I went to my own plane, which fortunately had escaped damage, I met Dr. Kubo. He had not been checked aboard the other planes as I had thought, and had just walked to the airport from his home, which was nearby. Before take-off there arrived copies of letters from General MacArthur's headquarters explaining the Joint Commission and requesting cooperation from the commanding generals of the Sixth and Eighth Armies. Since we were about to enter the Sixth Army command the letter was especially welcome.

We left at 11:10 A.M. in the third plane and had a smooth and pleasant flight, except for the fact that much of the land below was obscured by billowy and milky-white clouds. Finally we saw the shocking and breathtaking sight of Hiroshima below, devastated, cold—an ash. Our two C-46 predecessors were sitting like great olive-drab moths on the sandy yellow-gray field below. We flew over the harbor sighting the beautiful islands, and then made a rough landing with our tail too far up and not touching down quite soon enough. We taxied too far with our over-great momentum and landed in the mud but skirted around the worst parts, raising a great spray in the puddles, but we were able to come about to join our friends who were waiting. There was really no airport, no tower, no landing lights—only a wind sock. On the field were also some horribly scarred children, including a boy who told us in understandable English of his experience. He seemed to know how far he had been from the center of the explosion. In the meantime Major Kramer had made arrangements with the 186th Infantry Regiment to borrow a truck. The unloading was done without incident. They took a large wooden platform and placed it on a two-and-a-half-ton truck which was backed to the airplanes. The jeeps were then driven on and carried to a grassy revetment at the side of the airfield. Each jeep was finally bounced off with a jolt and then allowed to roll off the steep bank of the revetment. There seemed not to be too much immediate serious damage. We then rode through the bleakest scene that could be imagined—past a gray prison with blue-clad prisoners herded by blue-uniformed policemen. The entire city was completely flat except for some concrete buildings that looked reasonably well-preserved as we were landing and from a distance, but were all burned out and sometimes twisted and buckled masses upon closer view. The roads are still littered with wreckage of every description. There are many burned-out trucks and cars. Charred poles have collapsed, and jumbled wires crisscross the path. Most remarkable is the fact that through this scene of desolation streets cars are running through the middle of the devastated and almost empty city. Everywhere there is evidence of a conflagration. As we reach the margin of the city, many houses, although unburned, have been flattened, as if by wind, all in the same direction, away from the center of the explosion.

Our destination was Ujina. Here were the relatively intact living quarters of employees of the Daiwa rayon mill, some four-and-a-half kilometers from the center, which had been used as a hospital for care of the injured by personnel of the Tokyo First Military Hospital who were still in control. It was now almost dark. I went to the headquarters building and there in a small, dimly lighted room met Major Misono, who was in charge of the hospital. He was tall, rather dark, and had the look of a mainland Mongol. He was obviously weary and had a rough, scraggly black beard. He was curt and seemed almost surly, often saying "Wot?" in a rather gruff way when he did not quite understand, but soon he introduced us to Captain Sasano, who was much more suave. He then guided us to a building where we took three large well-lighted rooms, supplied with electric current. The buildings were long, two-storied, reminiscent of barracks in our own army, and arranged in cantonement style. They were, however, typical Japanese high-roofed structures supported by a heavy tree beam and with the typical Japanese sliding walls and doors. Our equipment was all stored after being unloaded from the truck and placed, with some attempt at separation of the categories of supplies, in a large room at the end of our building. The buildings branched off long, straight, covered walks.

We were now hungry. Sergeant Buckles was appointed mess officer and did the cooking over a gasoline stove. We had plenty of Ten-in-One rations, which make simple but tasty and adequate meals. At supper Jack Rosenbaum told the rest of us a blood-chilling tale of his experience on the flight down. When his plane reached altitude, one of the passengers, Dr. Yasuda, became extremely short of breath and cyanotic. Jack thought he might have had a coronary occlusion, until he found that Dr. Yasuda had a therapeutic pneumothorax which had expanded sufficiently to cause respiratory embarrassment as the plane ascended above 9,000 feet. Oxygen was administered, and the flight down was along the coast a few hundred feet above sea level.

The rooms had straw mats but there were, of course, no beds. We proceeded first to spray floor and walls liberally with DDT. A number of Japanese military blankets were obtained through Captain Sasano. These were clean, heavy, of a drab yellow-brown color, made of cot-

C O P Y

A.G.   500
12 October 1945

SUBJECT: Atomic Bomb Investigation.

TO   :   Commanding General, Sixth Army, APO 442.

1.   This headquarters has directed that a "Joint Commission for the Investigation of the Effects of the Atomic Bomb in Japan" conduct such investigations as are necessary. The commission is composed of the following three major groups.

       a.   The Manhattan Project Group under Brigadier General Farrell.

       b.   The GHQ Group under the Chief Surgeon's Office, represented by Colonel A. W. Oughterson, MC.

       c.   The Japanese Government Group under the direction of Dr. Tsuzuki of the Imperial University, Tokyo.

2.   It is desired that this commission be furnished whatever assistance is necessary and practicable in order to accomplish their mission. Colonel A. W. Oughterson is the plenary representative of the Joint Commission in Japan. Appropriate passes should be issued at his request to enable the parties to enter restricted areas of your command.

      FOR THE SUPREME COMMANDER:

                H. W. ALLEN,
                Colonel, A.G.D.,
                Asst Adjutant General.

A TRUE COPY

BRUCE J. WEBSTER,
Colonel, Medical Corps.

The order from General MacArthur establishing the Joint Commission. Although not included in this order, personnel of a unit serving with the U.S. Navy (Naval Technical Mission to Japan, Team 11) under Cmdr. Shields Warren worked in cooperation with the army unit at Nagasaki.

Hiroshima: an aerial view on landing, October 12, 1945. Only the heavily reinforced concrete buildings remain standing. To the right is the military area. The hypocenter is just to the left of the broad roadway which borders this area at its southern (left) margin. The two bank buildings, approximately 250 meters from the hypocenter, can be seen standing close together. The tall building near the lower left margin is the Fukuya department store.

Another aerial view taken on October 12. In the middle of the photograph is the burned zone of the city; beyond the broad highway, which acted as a firebreak, there is only scattered evidence of mechanical damage to buildings.

Above: A view across the hypocenter from Sanwa Bank. In the center is the Chamber of Commerce Building, with its domed tower. To the right is the Businessmen's Club (Korean Building). The low wall near the center represents the only portion of the Shima Private Hospital left standing.

Below: An adjacent view, looking farther north. The Korean Building is now in the center. To the right are the great white *torii* of the Gokoku shrine, 250 meters from the hypocenter, and close by is the military compound.

A general view of the city, looking toward the harbor. There is almost total destruction, with only a few walls of weight-bearing brick or concrete still standing.

The Chamber of Commerce Building before and after the bombing (300 meters).

ton, and singularly devoid of warmth. I had a sleeping bag with me which had traveled the long way from Camp Edwards to New Zealand to Saipan and now to Hiroshima. As soon as lights were out we heard a scurrying along the tree beams and hoped, even as we dozed off in exhaustion, that none of the rats, which sounded large, would become too inquisitive. The sleeping bag provided more comfort than was available for the rest, who were quite cold.

October 13, 1945: Early in the morning we inspected the establishment, found three large rooms in one of the buildings to be supplied with power and water, and designated them as the laboratory. Equipment and food were placed under the guard of our enlisted men, and Drs. Rosenbaum and Nakao were designated to unpack the laboratory equipment, to lay out a plan, and to gather what furniture could be found for the laboratory.

I drove to Kure with Colonel Mason to establish the necessary administrative framework with appropriate representatives of the Sixth Army. The drive, through only partly repaired roads, was rough and nervewracking. Considerable traffic, slowly moving trucks, and some military vehicles on the highway made progress very slow. On the way we picked up a young man named Yamashita who was working as an interpreter. He is one of the Los Angeles "double citizens" who had returned to Japan before 1941 and had apparently felt that Japan would be winning the war. He had gotten himself well-fixed for a post-war job, had Japan in fact been victorious. In the harbor of devastated Kure, which sloped steeply to the shore, there were many ships apparently unloading. We presented our orders to the adjutant general in the Tenth Corps headquarters, who introduced us to the provost marshall, Lieutenant Colonel Pence. He was a stern-looking but kindly, graying gentleman who quickly supplied us with the necessary passes, but said that they would be valid only until the end of the month, when they could be renewed at ASCOM. This headquarters had not as yet been fully established. The Hiroshima area had been made off-limits because of careless behavior and looting by souvenir hunters. These were men of the merchant marine who would come into the harbor in boats, keeping a sharp lookout for mines, and then quickly depart. Only supervised groups were permitted to enter to view the city, and, of course, those on official business.

Then tried to call upon Colonel Hall, the surgeon. We found him on an inspection tour out of his office. Here we met Major Cummings, who had been the executive officer to Colonel Carton, whom I had met on Espiritu Santo in the New Hebrides. Major Cummings was now serving as executive officer to Colonel Mudgett, the base surgeon. For old times' sake he said that he had a whole case of VO whiskey which he was willing to share. This offer was accepted with alacrity. We paid our respects to Major Hamlin, Colonel Hall's

An aerial view of the Daiwa Rayon Mill in Ujina, used as a hospital by the Tokyo First Military Hospital and later by the Joint Commission. The dormitory buildings of the factory, which were used for the hospital, are in the upper center of the photograph.

The entrance to the Ujina Hospital, with military personnel still on duty and patients.

executive officer, and then visited the 361st Station Hospital near Kure. Unfortunately, the site selected for this hospital was waterless, and this had caused understandable dismay among the personnel. Later in the afternoon we went to the Japanese prefectural office to see whether better lodgings could be obtained for our operation at Hiroshima, but it was clear that adequate facilities were not available. We therefore set about to find civilian assistance for cooking and laundry, which was quickly accomplished with the help of Dr. Murachi. Before returning, we visited also the 186th Infantry Regiment, where Lieutenant Farrell agreed to service our jeeps. Since these were newly arrived directly from the hot and dusty Philippines without attention, they were in obvious need.

On our return we found that the laboratory was already getting into shape under the ministrations of Drs. Rosenbaum and Nakao, who had been busy all day. I also found, to my relief, that Dr. Ishii had arrived by train. It was now decided that we would no longer keep guards on our food supply. Our Japanese colleagues told us that absolutely nothing would be touched even though there were many people in dire need. This released both Ohnstadt and Huffaker, who with Sergeants Reed and Buckles set to work with a will. Dr. Ishii's arrival now made our group complete as finally planned just before departing Tokyo:

Americans	*Japanese*
Col. Verne R. Mason	Dr. Kanshi Sassa
Lieut. Col. Averill A. Liebow	Dr. Kiku Nakao
Maj. Milton R. Kramer	Dr. Koichi Murachi
Capt. Calvin O. Koch	Dr. Shuichi Kato
Capt. Jack D. Rosenbaum	Dr. Toru Tsukada
1st Lieut. J. Philip Loge	Dr. Ikuya Kubo
T/Sgt. John P. Reed	Dr. Tamaki Kajitani
S/Sgt. Hial D. Huffaker	Dr. Koichi Ishikawa
T/4 James E. Buckles	Dr. Takeshi Gotoh
Pvt. Michas Ohnstadt	Dr. Shigeru Hatano
	Dr. Moto Kawanoura
	Dr. Toshiaki Yasuda
	Dr. Hirotake Kakehi
	Dr. Masaaki Okoshi
	Dr. Zenichiro Ishii

There were also twenty-one medical students, including Mr. Shimamine, who came at the request of Dr. Ishii. Major Misono was in charge of the hospital, and Major Motohashi was also assigned there, although we had not yet met him. Dr. Tsuzuki and Colonel Oughterson had not arrived but expected to divide their time between Hiroshima, Nagasaki, and Tokyo.

To bed, with some of Major Cummings' VO to soothe us.

October 14: Arose on a very cold Sunday morning after a quite comfortable night in my sleeping bag-rubber mattress arrangement. At 9:00 A.M., conferred with the Japanese physicians. It was decided that Dr. Sassa as the senior among the Japanese and Colonel Mason as our senior officer should undertake a goodwill mission to meet the doctors of the various hospitals and of the Prefecture. It was decided to postpone this undertaking since Sundays are taken quite seriously in these parts. We used most of the day in putting the laboratory into a quite functional state. During the day copper sulfate solutions for plasma and blood specific-gravity determinations were prepared by Captain Rosenbaum. I spent a good deal of my time, with assistance of our sergeants and some of the Japanese, preparing oxalate tubes for collecting blood and dehydrating solutions for histology. Fortunately there was power of the proper voltage for our centrifuges and waterbaths. We had not been sure of this when the equipment was brought down.

Late in the evening we had a second consultation to crystallize plans for actual work. It seemed expedient to work up the Ujina patients first and then to proceed to hospitalized patients elsewhere. Survey work on the non-hospitalized population would be conducted in clinics later. A laboratory team was organized consisting of Drs. Nakao and Okoshi and myself, to be assisted by a number of junior men and students. Clinical teams were organized in five units. This was greeted with enthusiasm by all concerned. Our record forms were considered again in great detail in an effort to be certain that there would be no mistakes in interpretation. It was decided that the data from the clinical examinations would be recorded on the Japanese forms and then transcribed so that both the English and Japanese records would be complete. Laboratory data, when available, were to be entered on each. This principle of duplication and sharing of

UNITED STATES ARMED FORCES

PROVOST MARSHAL PASS   NO. 886____
(Temporary)
                      X Corps
        Location _____

Please   Permit   Col B. R. Mason   Atomic Bomb Survey
                  & driver or member of
                  Name atomic bomb   Address or Organization
                        commission,
         entrance to ____Hiroshima_____
                            Army Installation or Area

         for purpose   Study of the effects of the atomic bomb.
                     State exact mission & unit or person concerned

         12 November 1945   12 December 1945   THESE PERSONNEL WILL BE
From _____ _____ to _____ _____   ALLOWED TO ENTER AND
       hour   date   hour   date   LEAVE HIROSHIMA AT ANY
                                                     TIME OF DAY OR NIGHT.
                                   Approved   12 November 1945   ____
                                              Date
Cleared by_____   Provost Marshal_____

_____ CIC Det   X Corps Capt. Corp of Military Pol.
                                   Organization or Area

A military pass required for entry into the Hiroshima area.

the material was to allay any suspicion that we would simply use the
material for our own purposes and that the Japanese would be kept
from making a study and from publishing on their own. All appeared most eager to begin the actual work on the morrow.

October 15: In the early morning again had a meeting with the
teams, who arranged themselves according to plan for the work
with the Ujina Hospital in-patients. The clinical teams went to work
questioning and examining the patients. An assigned case number
was left at the bedside for the laboratory team so that specimens
would be properly marked. The laboratory collecting team, consisting
of Drs. Okoshi and Nakao and Sergeants Reed and Buckles, followed along, obtaining blood and other specimens. This system
worked out well although the laboratory group tended to lag somewhat behind. It was remarkable to see the patients lying or sitting
about on the straw mats of the small rooms. There were no beds.
Numerous fires were burning in the charcoal stoves everywhere. Many
women were present, apparently relatives of patients to whom they

ministered, but there were also nurses, wearing *mompé*, white blouses
and pancake-shaped hats marked in front by a little red cross. We
learned that it was Japanese custom for kinfolk to serve patients and
even to cook for them while they were in the hospital. Many of the
patients were horribly burned and others had various crude but effec-
tive orthopedic appliances. They seemed entirely docile and showed
no evidence of hostility, but rather a submissive courteousness.
There was a remarkable absence of odor, despite the open infected
wounds and burns and pitiful condition of some of the patients.

To us the treatment seemed deficient, in that little attention to
electrolyte balance and adequate fluid therapy had been paid.
Transfusions in our sense were almost nonexistent. The closest approach was the injection of blood in quantities of 50 cc. into the
muscle of the buttocks—and the blood was usually derived from
the patient himself. German field medicine was said to have exhibited
the same deficiencies. The Japanese pharmaceutical industry had
successfully reached the sulfapyridine production stage, but even this
material was apparently not used in large quantities. The earliest
stages of penicillin production also had been attained in Japan, but
we were told that this material was available only in small quantities
and was rarely used, and then only in very small doses. This was
probably fortunate since the product then was still quite toxic. By
late afternoon all of the Ujina patients had been seen and the teams
returned triumphantly to the laboratory rooms, which served as a
meeting place.

On returning from the wards we have dinner prepared from the
excellent Ten-in-One rations by an accommodating Japanese cook
variously called Perlmutter or Rochester. He is efficient, quick to
learn, and obviously enjoys his job, since he is the recipient of what
to others seems like manna, which he obviously takes home to share
with his family. All of us are now free of the chores of housekeeping
and can devote ourselves fully to the job at hand. On this first evening we all gather together, transcribe the completed records, and
enter laboratory data that have been obtained in the meantime. All
seem quite satisfied with the operation and with the opportunity
to do systematic and creative work.

For numbering and identifying the records I devised a system
whereby the prefix *H* was to indicate the hospitalized cases, *O* out-
patients, and *S* persons to be used in a survey. A block of numbers

Left: One of the workers' dormitory buildings at the Daiwa Rayon Mill in Ujina, used as a laboratory by the Joint Commission.

Right: Professor Tsuzuki in one of the corridors at the Ujina Hospital.

A group from the laboratory of the Joint Commission at Ujina. Four of the nurses who assisted in the preparation of the glassware are shown. The physicians are, from left to right, Dr. Kato, Dr. Kajitani (at rear), Dr. Nakao, Lieut. J. Philip Loge, Dr. Tsukada, and Dr. Okoshi. Professor Tsuzuki's confidence in these men is borne out by the positions they have attained since the end of the war: Dr. Nakao is professor of internal medicine at Tokyo University, and Dr. Kajitani is chief of surgery at the Cancer Institute. Two others, Drs. Ishikawa and Hatano, are now professors of surgery at Tokyo University.

beginning with 6,000 was reserved for the individual Hiroshima patients, and a suffix was added to indicate the source of the record. For the Ujina patients we used the suffix U. The old Ujina cases in the group from which Dr. Nakao had bone marrow and peripheral blood were given the first block of numbers, H-6,000U to H-6,044U. The records of these patients were available at the Ujina Hospital. In fact, among those examined today were identified patients who had had previous marrow punctures in the Nakao series. These were especially valuable in terms of follow-up, and there was general agreement regarding the desirability of second marrow punctures, which were therefore planned. These might provide evidence of recovery in marrows where there had previously been leukopenia.

Colonel Mason and Dr. Sassa had been establishing liaison with other hospitals in and near Hiroshima as they had planned. It seemed best to send teams next to the Prefectural Hospital and to the outpatient clinic at the Post Office Hospital, where Dr. Hachiya, the gracious director, welcomed them. Drs. Rosenbaum and Koch were to go to the former in the morning, to be followed by Phil Loge and the laboratory team in the afternoon. Colonel Mason and Major Kramer, with a group of the Japanese students, were to go to the Post Office Hospital.

In discussion with Colonel Mason, we concluded that my own function for now would be to remain at home base for a time, to maintain the laboratory and bring it into a functional state for preparing histological sections, to systematize and keep the records, to establish a flow chart of work to be done, to schedule the work for the clinical teams, and in free time to continue the translations of autopsy protocols and records from the hospitalized patients seen earlier at various institutions. Colonel Mason said that he preferred to continue with the work of establishing contacts with the Japanese medical institutions, to maintain liaison with headquarters at Kure, and to function as supply officer. He would obtain from the chief medical officers in the Japanese institutions accounts of the numbers and kinds of patients and their findings and experience with them. He was also particularly interested in effects on the eyes and would make a special effort to obtain accurate data. He would rely on us to carry on with the rest of the labor.

October 16: The teams departed by jeep for their destinations immediately after breakfast.

Post Office Hospital —

Is about 1.2 Km from our center. We this building in this reinforced concrete building. About 80 people were in the building and many of those (85%) were injured. Only one died later of cuts from glass. Bomb at 8:05 A.M. and soon — about 9 A.M. 50 pts came here — the fire had not yet started — then patients kept coming in — about 400 on the first and about 200 of these waited outside. All together about 5000 patients were seen or admitted. Many had burns and died of the burns. Many died the first 3-4 days with fever, nausea, vomiting and diarrhoea and many of these died of water-loss. None had water by vein the first 2-3 days. Later some had salt solution without good effect. No medicine was here then because of the destruction

Above and right: Notes made by Colonel Mason at an interview with Dr. M. Hachiya, director of the Communications Department (Post Office) Hospital. Dr. Hachiya later published his detailed *Hiroshima Diary.*

of their supplies. Dr. Hachiya was injured in his house in area 4 — 1.3 Km from center. He didn't hear the noise but he saw the light. His + his wife's WBC got down to 3000. per mm³. They did not have epilation. The house had a tile roof. Wasser-mangel was from nausea + vomiting but also because there was neither water nor food to be obtained after the fire started.

At 9:00, soon after they had gone, Dr. Miyazaki, one of a group of Japanese scientists who had been studying radiation effects in the city, came and presented data concerning how the center point of the explosion was determined to be 547 meters above the ground. He gave a graphic description of the shadows, some of which had both an umbra and a penumbra, and of the process of triangulation. He also suggested that the Koimachi district might be the source of secondary radiation, perhaps on account of the water's having acquired radioactive properties. He told also of a secondary focus of radiation resulting from the fall of radioactive dust in the Takasu area.

I then began to work on the first batch of the now-completed records of the patients in the group collected by Dr. Nakao. These were translated word-for-word for entry into the general series. About noontime I was pleased to find that Colonel Oughterson and Dr. Tsuzuki had arrived from Tokyo with a little mail for us. It was a delight to hear from my parents and from C. G., now in Maine. It was a peculiar pleasure also to have a newspaper in hand. We then informed him about our work to date, which seemed to be progressing

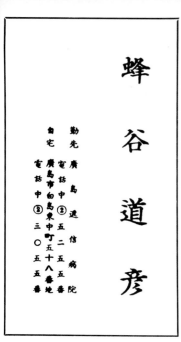

michihiko

M. Hachiya

Master of Hiroshima

Teishin Hospital.

Dr. Hachiya's card and signature.

smoothly, and our attempts to locate as much of the material as possible. He promised to attempt to get us more transportation, which is our chief deficiency at the present time.

Our Japanese chef, Perlmutter, was preparing lunch as Colonel Oughterson arrived, much to the latter's pleasure.

During the afternoon Dr. Kato and I went to the wards, and I observed the Japanese technique of vertebral spinous-process marrow puncture. It was most impressive. A No. 19 plain needle was used. In two motions the skin was penetrated to the bone and the needle tapped through the thin cortical shell into the marrow cavity. In another, suction was applied and a small quantity of what looked like blood drawn into the syringe. We later stained the smears and found them to be remarkably rich in marrow cells, as was the case with the material that I had seen previously in Tokyo in the patients without aplastic anemia.

For the first time also I was able to view some of the postmortem material that had been promised by Dr. Ishii. The slides were well prepared and were well selected from all significant organs. There was also considerable gross material. Unfortunately much of this was fixed in rather small quantities of formalin and may be not as useful for study as the small blocks that have already been prepared. We planned to attempt to restore some of the color and to photograph the specimens on 35-mm. color film.

I had noted that Dr. Ishii had worn only sandals despite the cold and wet. On impulse I asked whether he would like an extra pair of shoes that I had along, if they would fit. I was able to gather that he would, and presented them to him privately.

October 17: In the morning, very early, met Dr. Hayashi, a professor emeritus of pharmacology at the Imperial University of Tokyo. He was a most impressive, dignified, white-haired man, alert and keen despite his seventy-one years. He had been a teacher of both Dr. Tsuzuki and Dr. Sassa. I explained to him how the work was progressing, discussed plans, and asked for his suggestions. He was most gracious.

The team working at the Prefectural Hospital now has almost finished the work. There have been several important developments. We have an ambulance, and a driver, Spears, has been added to our staff. Colonel Mason has been foraging, and a number of additional sleeping bags have somehow been provided—but there are only three, and some of the senior officers are unhappy.

Dr. Murachi, our biophysicist, gave an interesting hint of secondary radiation effects. A man who had returned several days after the bombing to a concrete building had had a transient leukopenia. We said that much more evidence would have to be gathered before any cause-and-effect relationship would be established. Dr. Murachi agreed and stressed that neutrons might have induced sufficient secondary radioactivity to have given the observed result.

[Observations of this sort at Hiroshima were isolated, and the leukopenia may have had some other cause. Members of a military unit, the Ishizuka Regiment, had camped from August 6 to 11 in the near vicinity of the hypocenter, at Kamiya-cho. Blood counts done by the Japanese before the end of August showed no evidence of leukopenia. This well-established observation and physical measurements indicated that there was no biologically significant neutron-induced secondary radiation at Hiroshima.]

During the afternoon several of the autopsy cases were translated by Dr. Ishii from the Japanese. I transcribed them and later in the evening dictated the transcripts to Private Ohnstadt.

October 18: Teams with Major Kramer and Dr. Rosenbaum assigned to Red Cross Hospital. Joined them there about mid-morning. Met the vice director, Dr. Shigeto, who is understandably sad and discouraged. Had an extensive tour of what must have been a fine modern hospital. Rooms and equipment have been unbelievably damaged and there are many patients, again attended by their families, amid shattered surroundings. Buckled metal window-frames and broken plaster exposing lathwork are everywhere, although an attempt has been made to clear the debris.

On returning, continued translation of protocols with Dr. Ishii. Later in the morning two photographers, Ware and Circus, appeared. These men were on loan from local headquarters until our photography unit was assigned. Also Lieutenant Vance, Sanitary Corps, a parasitologist, has been attached. He seems a very nice sort and brings along a welcome item—another microscope. To my amazement and pleasure, two more microscopes arrived with Colonel Mason, who had obtained them on loan from the Twenty-ninth Malaria Survey Detachment. He also brought a radio from the I & E section of Tenth Corps headquarters (now we would again be in immediate contact with the outside world!) and, best of all, said that a refrigerator, six cubic feet, Frigidaire no less, was waiting to be picked up at the 411th Medical Collecting Company. The 361st Station Hospital had furnished a uterine curette and an ophthalmoscope. He accepted our enthusiastic compliments without blushing and said it was all the result of his eagles screaming.

In the afternoon Colonel Oughterson brought in an X-ray film which had been exposed during the burst of radioactivity and whose location was known. This had also been seen previously by members of the Manhattan District group, and by the highly competent radiologist Major Misono (who had been in command of the hospital when we arrived). We discussed again at length the shielding and protection problem with Dr. Murachi and Major Misono, who had been interested from the beginning and had given these matters much thought. In fact this was one of Dr. Murachi's prime interests. We planned a thorough tour of the city tomorrow in order that I might have the benefit of his previous observations and thinking.

In the evening there was a lecture by Dr. Kitaoka of Okayama, attended by all. He said that the tuberculin reactions and Schick skin tests were diminished among exposed patients in whom there had been leukopenic reaction.

D. M. Fumio Shigeto,

Vice director of Red Cross Hospital
Hiroshima Japan

Dr. Shigeto's card and signature.

October 19, 1945: In the morning, took a trip with Dr. Murachi to the city in the region of the hypocenter. Dr. Murachi had a detailed knowledge of the noteworthy and most revealing physical features. Ascended the stairs of the burned-out Sanwa Bank to the roof. The reinforced concrete walls were solid, but many of the partitions had been fragmented and the wood supporting the plaster had burned, as had the furnishings. In one room *sake* cups were still on the floor amid the rubble. The roof of the Sanwa, only 500 meters from the hypocenter, is one of the best places from which to view the city, as one can see over the hypocenter itself toward the remarkable domed building which the Japanese call the Commercial Museum (Chamber of Commerce). We measured the thickness of the walls of the Sanwa. As we went to the former Mitsui (Teihoku) Bank, there was still the smell of death, and the burned bones of a dead man were visible, trapped deep within the rubble. Remarkably, the walls of the structure itself showed no evidence of burning. On the ground were many tiles, and in the small cemeteries, of which there were many, were the vases made of *setomono*. At the hypocenter itself trees were upright but leafless and charred. Nearby were the ruins of a brick building which Dr. Murachi identified as the Shima Hospital. This had been of weight-bearing brick, which had completely collapsed. The day was ideal for a photograph, which I took from in front of the hospital across the hypocenter toward the two impressive bank buildings and the ruin of the Bankers' Club. As we were walking about, Major Hamlin drove up in a command car to tell us that a photographic team was expected at the Hiroshima airfield later in the day. They were to be assigned to us for the duration and had been asked to bring their equipment with them. We watched the vicinity of the airfield while examining the various buildings, but saw no aircraft.

We then drove the short distance to the broad road between the main city and the border of the military reservation. On the west side was the Gokoku shrine, where the most remarkable shadows on the granite, and also the interval between the heat wave and blast wave were demonstrated. Nearby was a high modern building, again with a sound outer structure but blasted and burned within. People had taken rooms in this building for living quarters; now completely windowless, it had been screened with rough woven mats. Dr. Murachi told me that they were Koreans who had always felt downtrodden but now considered themselves victors over the Japanese and therefore entitled to the best quarters. On the topmost landing Dr. Murachi showed me some remarkable shadows of the metal railing and upright edge of the building on the horizontal cement slab which supported the former. The shadows consisted of dark, gray-brown streaks corresponding to the horizontals and verticals, surrounded by a vaguely defined rusty-brown band. The darker portions represent the umbra, which still had the grimy appearance closer to that of the original cement, while the part that had been directly exposed to the heat had a clean white appearance. The part between, which was rusty brown, represented the penumbra and therefore the effect of a lesser degree of heat. Murachi complained that the shadows were fading and that good photographic records must be made at once. From the same landing we could look across to the dome of the Commercial Museum. Here the unbelievable effect of the blast was evident, since a concrete wall had been made concave and a roof converted into a saucer by the downward and lateral force. The most remarkable shadows were on the Bantai Bridge at 1,000 meters from the hypocenter, where not only the railing of the bridge but also outlines of people were plainly visible on the asphalt. Farther from the center of the city, near the middle

The face of the monument at the Gokuku shrine, 300 meters from the hypocenter. The directly exposed portions of the granite have become roughened and flaky, while the portion of the base shaded by the upright edge retains the original polish, producing a shadow.

A similar effect on the base of the granite rail. The blast wave knocked down the uprights at a time when the heat of the flash had become so reduced that the original appearance of the monument was retained. This demonstrates the difference between the rates of propagation of the heat wave and the blast wave.

of the bridge, was the clear outline of a hand cart and of the person who had apparently been pulling it. These "shadows" were of a lighter color than the remainder of the asphalt, which had been darkened by the heat flash. During this remarkable tour we discussed possibilities for the protection studies. Dr. Murachi said that there were official reports on survivors in the City Hall and of employees in the large utility buildings which would give crude data for comparison with survival of persons in certain wooden buildings, but that much very careful work would have to be done to establish the exact position of individuals.

[It is astonishing, and a tribute to the resiliency of the people, that even at this early time the city was showing signs of revival. When we first arrived there was almost no one to be seen. The trolley cars that rumbled through the streets amid the ruins were almost empty. A few crude shelters had been put together from the rubble, but these were unoccupied. There was dread of the imminent arrival of the unknown conqueror, occasioned by inconsiderate treatment on the part of a few who had entered the area before. But now not only were people moving back from the villages where they had been staying with relatives and friends, but bamboo scaffolding was beginning to appear on some of the larger buildings. Life in the crowded surrounding towns was active. Clothing and other goods made locally seemed abundant, and even cheaply manufactured articles were on display. Food was scarce, less so in the more distant villages, and rationing was still in force. The rice crop was ripening even in the close environs of Hiroshima. The attitude was definitely no longer one of paralysis but one of encouragement and hope despite privation.]

Upon returning to the laboratory, met Major Motohashi. He was a very small, bright-eyed, sharp-jawed, active young man who gave the appearance of high intelligence. He had a fluent command of English, which he spoke in a high-pitched voice. He said that there might be patients at the Niho Hospital, whereupon I dispatched him and Captain Rosenbaum to investigate. With Ishii and the two photographers who had been assigned previously on loan, photographed a great many specimens that might be used to illustrate our report. They used a Graphic news camera and I made the photo-

Left: A shadow on the prison wall at Hiroshima (2,3000 meters).

Right: The shadow of a rail on concrete at the Businessmen's Club (Korean Building). There is a darker central portion, representing the umbra, and a more vaguely defined periphery representing the penumbra (350 meters).

Left: The light-colored shadows of a window frame. The wood has been charred where it was directly exposed, even through glass. The shadow represents the original color of the material.

Right: The shadow of a ladder on a gas tank at 2,200 meters. The shadow represents the original color of the tank, which has been lightened by direct exposure to the rays. Other shadows are also seen on the tank.

graphs in parallel with color film and a 35-mm. Leica. We photographed lungs, intestines, heart, bones, kidneys, and other organs. It had been possible to refresh the color of the organs somewhat with 80 per cent alcohol since they had faded during their long fixation in formalin.

Late in the afternoon discovered that it was bath day and promptly repaired to the communal pool at the far end of the Ujina living quarters. This is perhaps a quarter of a mile down the long covered arcades, where there is a large building that itself looks like a factory unit. It has a smokestack from which gray and black smoke belches. Inside all is laughter and good cheer. The pool itself can accommodate perhaps 75 at one time at an arm's length apart. The custom is to have a complete scrub before entering the pool. This is done by filling a small wooden tub with the hot water, wetting and soaping oneself down, rinsing, and, when clean, entering the water at the cooler end. "Cooler" means just barely tolerable to Caucasian skin. At the far corner live steam bubbles through the water. I was amazed to see habitués standing almost at that very point. To the uninitiated the approach must be very gradual. In the pool conversation is animated. Everyone is relaxed. Gossip and jokes are exchanged. Both the atmosphere and the temperature thaw reserve, and one emerges with friendly feelings for everyone and everything, including cold, gray weather. We had heard tales of how in the villages people walk naked from such a bath through wintry streets without harm. Actually the warm pleasant glow remains for some hours after such a bath. At Ujina it is available twice a week. I resolve then never to miss an opportunity. After a good supper from Uncle Sam's Ten-in-One supply it is actually pleasant to get back to work in the evening. Work is now in full swing, and no one can get to bed before midnight; we must rise before 6:30 to embark on the day's activities. We now have four Japanese nurses who clean glassware and prepare everything for the next day after we get to bed and who always are in the laboratory when we arrive. Since our coming there has not been a moment to spare as we feel the opportunities of observing patients still at the height of illness is quickly disappearing. The last event in the day for me is always to complete this diary.

[At this time our Japanese hosts favored us with an act of great kindness. The usual facility for elimination, the *benjo*, consists of a graceful but narrow bowl built close to the ground, designed not to touch the skin but to be squatted over. The more modern devices are provided with facilities for flushing, but this convenience had not yet been provided the workers' barracks in the Daiwa Rayon Mill. Having heard of the Western custom, the officers ordered the construction of what they thought were appropriate settees. This task was efficiently and handsomely accomplished—with a single major difficulty. Although the orifice was of reasonable dimensions, the seat, rather than being built like a bench, had been made like a saddle, at right angles to the proper direction! The matter was duly rectified, with considerable hilarity on both sides.]

October 20: In the morning, as I was working away at translations, in came a Caucasian woman, Mrs. Yamatoda, with a Mr. Suga, an English-speaking friend. She told a long story of how her husband had died during the war after marrying her in 1926. At that time she was left with her relatives, who were hostile, especially a former Japanese Naval man. All I could do was to promise that I would have her brought to the Red Cross at headquarters, where she could present her case.

The problem of food for our Japanese colleagues again came up in a lengthy discussion with Dr. Sassa. They had been supplied from our stock of military rations (headquarters had given a hesitant blessing), but complained that they found the diet too rich to be agreeable and that they required adequate quantities of their staple, rice. As Professor Sassa put it in no uncertain terms, "Japanese people must have rice!" Knowing that rice was still strictly rationed in Japan I inquired what had become of their ration cards. He was somewhat evasive but gradually it came out, more from his colleagues than himself, that many of the cards had been left with the families in the Tokyo area. They had evidently thought that their own problems would be solved, and that their families might have the benefit of their own cards. After discussing the matter with Colonel Oughterson we decided that the best solution under the circumstances would simply be to demand the rice from the local authorities. I therefore went to the prefectural office near Kaitaichi and, stern-faced but polite, requested the rice. Conversation with the somewhat bewildered officer was difficult and was conducted through an interpreter. He finally agreed that we could have the rice

The shadow of a person on the Bantai Bridge (1,000 meters), outlined in chalk. The asphalt has been darkened by exposure to the flash. Further down the bridge is the outline of a cart and the person drawing it.

Captain Brownell standing over the shadow in the position of the person who was standing there at the moment of the explosion.

The outline of the cart and the person drawing it, seen from above. Further to the right are the outlines of other persons who were on the bridge.

if I were to sign for it. This I of course agreed to do, and we made off with several hundred pounds of the grain quickly, hoping that nothing untoward would happen.

After the day's work our Japanese colleagues suggested that we spend tomorrow (Sunday) on Miyajima, a famous shrine island in the Inland Sea nearby. We agreed that a day of relaxation was highly indicated.

Sunday, October 21: After a hearty breakfast on this crisp clear day we crowded everyone into all of our available vehicles, including the ambulance, and headed south along the coast toward Hatsukaichi. All then boarded the ferry to the beautiful deep-green hilly island across the sparkling water. As we approached the island we glimpsed just offshore the great *torii* standing high in the water. Beautiful temples lined the shore, and many of these were over the water, reached by cat-walks. After inspecting these we walked through the fall woods. The colors were beautiful but more subdued than those of New England, with many dark bronze or purple-red cut-leaved maples. From the heights there were occasional views of the sea and of other islands. Many people brought their cameras, and photography of everything in sight was in progress. One of our friends pointed to a sign and laughed. It said that this was a restricted military area and photography was forbidden—a message now obsolete. Our colleagues chose a restaurant deep in the hills for a mid-afternoon meal. The restaurant was located in a lovely rambling Japanese country house. Shoes were left outside among a forest of others. The *tatami* (mats) were spotless and one sat or squatted on them at low tables. The menu was carefully chosen by our friends. With a little warm *sake*, reserve was cast aside, faces flushed, conversation became animated and personal. The *sake* surely is only a formality to make this possible since the effect cannot be from the small quantity of alcohol. Everything was gracefully served by charming kimono-clad ladies. The dinner lasted several hours and there seemed to be plenty of food from raw fish to mushroom and meat dishes served with mountains of rice, and with plenty of *sake* and tea. I was uncertain whether the abundance indicated something illicit about the establishment in those days of stringency. We returned home through the sunset and dusk with a much better acquaintance with persons and a better feeling of the country.

At a meeting in the evening we discussed with the Japanese members methods for performing the survey study in order to obtain some idea of the distribution of effects around the hypocenter in relation to distance. Since there had been complete dislocation of the population and large numbers of people had died or had moved, or were otherwise unavailable, it was obviously not possible to obtain a representative sample. Still, a survey of survivors would disclose those with minor injuries and would give some idea of the distribution and severity of burns under various conditions of protection, and, to an extent, even of radiation effects. Some of us are particularly interested in amenorrhea. Dr. Mitani of the obstetrical department has made a study of this in Tokyo and states that there was clearly such a thing as "war amenorrhea" and that the study would have to be carefully controlled. The distance from the hypocenter would represent a determining factor. Standard record forms were to be prepared for each person in the survey, as for the hospitalized patients, and every fifth person was to have a complete blood count. The Japanese told us that the best way would be to approach the police officers and ask them to have people brought into the clinics and aid stations which were located in outlying parts of the city and in the nearby communities. The point was to obtain for examination numbers of persons who had been in all sectors and who had survived with minor injuries. I would keep a central record on one of the sector maps to be sure that roughly equal numbers were ultimately obtained from all sectors. Colonel Mason, Majors Motohashi and Misono, and other senior members of the group would make the contacts with the police officers and explain what was required.

October 22: Teams were dispatched to the smaller hospitals at Eba and Oshiba and to the out-patient clinics at the Red Cross and Post Office Hospitals. The twenty students who have arrived were sent with the teams to the out-patient departments to receive indoctrination, especially in questioning the patients and in filling out the record forms properly.

At the request of Drs. Nakao and Kato, discussed the follow-up work on former patients in the early Ujina (Nakao) series. They had been delving into the records and found that several of the discharged soldiers in that group were living in small communities near Hiroshima. We decided to attempt to locate them tomorrow. Both Nakao and Kato were confident that these people could be found.

They would prepare for hematological work-up and spinous-process puncture.

Later went with Colonel Mason and an interpreter to the Hiroshima West police station, where we met Chief Suzawa in his rather impressive office. He was cordial and gave the impression of brisk efficiency. We explained that we wanted a good cross-section of the population of both sexes and all ages who had been in various parts of the city at the moment of the explosion and who had been displaced and were now living in the area under his jurisdiction. He offered full cooperation, stating that it would not be difficult since all persons were registered. We arranged for a visit by our teams on the twenty-sixth at 9:30 A.M. During the day we visited several other stations and made similar arrangements to see from 150 to 200 persons.

Returned to continue translations and to work in the laboratory.

October 23: The out-patient work was continued in the major hospitals, and a team was sent to the Ajina Aid Station. Continued with the protocol translations. Section cutting and staining was now progressing superbly under the ministrations of Drs. Ishii and Shimamine. I noticed that the former sometimes now wore the shoes, but nothing was said. I could not resist going over some of the slides as they were finished.

When one of the jeeps returned, drove into the country with the Japanese physicians and Phil Loge. It was fascinating to see the rice —dry, brown, full of grain, and ready for the harvest. After considerable searching, and inquiry of men in the fields and paddies, we found two of the patients. We were graciously received and served tea on the matted back platform of the farm houses. Mr. Hiroshi Okita was actually at work on his farm. He was one of the survivors who had had rather extensive clinical and hematological studies twice previously while a patient at the Ujina Hospital (Case No. H-6011-U) and had been investigated by physicians of the Tokyo Dai Ichi Military Hospital. We had studied two previous marrow specimens with Dr. Nakao. Mr. Okita, then a soldier, had been in the upper floor of a two-story Japanese building in the barracks of the 104th Garrison Force at approximately 1,000 meters from the hypocenter. He was only slightly injured by flying glass and debris and was able to work and to march for the first ten days after the explosion. Beginning on August 20 he began to lose his hair. A week

地方警視　須澤良隆

宇品警察署長

Yoshitaka Suzawa
Chief of West
Police Department
Hiroshima City

Police Chief Suzawa's card and signature.

later he developed fever, petechiae, and swelling of the gums which became painful and hemorrhagic and ultimately ulcerated. He also developed sore throat and difficulty in swallowing. He was admitted to Ujina on August 30. His white blood count had been 900 on September 4, but rose to 1,400 by September 8 and to 4,600 by September 27 while he was a patient at the Ujina Hospital. He also had a marked anemia. The cell count of his bone marrow had been only 4,000 on September 4, with approximately half of the cells in the marrow being lymphocytes or plasma cells. In the second specimen, obtained on September 27, there was evidence of almost total recovery, except that there was now a relative hyperplasia of normoblasts. Today he appears well and states that he is able to work, although he becomes tired easily. His hair has largely grown back. There are still dark red-brown discolorations of his gums, but the ulcers have healed and are no longer painful. He submitted to the marrow puncture with alacrity. We found that his white blood cell count was 10,400 and that his marrow cell count was 75,000/mm³. The cellular constitution of the marrow was now normal. Despite his healthy

A view across the hypocenter toward the domed Chamber of Commerce Building (center distance). In the right distance is the Businessmen's Club (Korean Building). In the foreground are the Bankers' Club (left) and a bank building (right).

A part of the north wing of the Chamber of Commerce Building showing "dishing" of the flat roof as a result of the blast.

The shadows of a railing and of a person on the asphalt of the Bantai Bridge, approximately 1,000 meters from the hypocenter. The directly exposed asphalt has been darkened. Sighting along the shadows, in line with the objects which cast them, enabled Japanese scientists to locate the hypocenter by triangulation within a few days of the explosion.

Effects of the heat flash at 1,300 meters: sharp shadows of the leaves of a castor plant on a blackened telephone pole near the Meiji Bridge (1,300 meters). The plant at one time was taller, but the leaves which cast the shadow wilted where they were directly exposed to the heat rays. The rays were directed downward from a point approximately 625 meters above the hypocenter. The photograph was made on October 31, 1945.

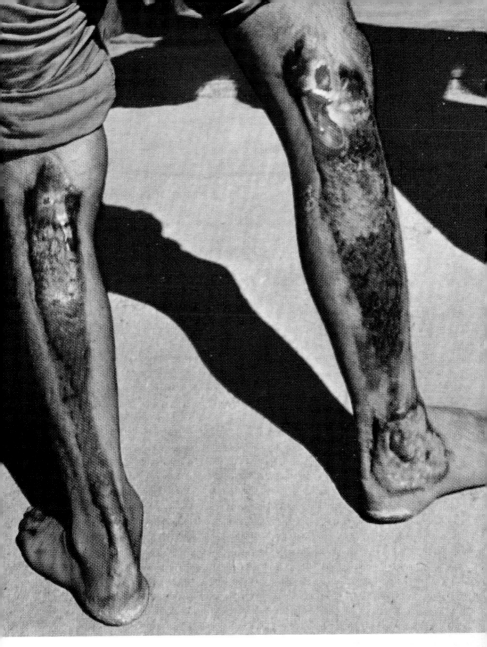

Profile burns of the legs. Only the directly exposed skin has been burned. There is evidence of keloid formation. The patient was a soldier in the military compound, approximately 900 meters from the hypocenter. (Enlargement of a 35-mm. transparency.)

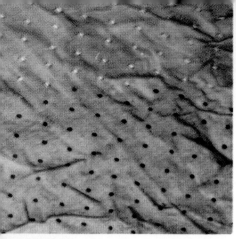

Section of garment made of light-colored cloth with a pattern of dark-colored dots. The dots that were directly exposed to the explosion of the atomic bomb absorbed infrared radiation and burned. The areas on the patient's body adjacent to these dots were also burned.

Close-up illustrating appearance of "ray burn" keloid formation as it appeared ninety-nine days after the explosion over Hiroshima. Note the coppery tissue at the center of the area and dark-reddish-brown hyperpigmented zone along the margins.

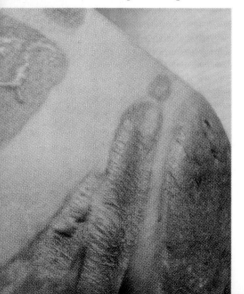

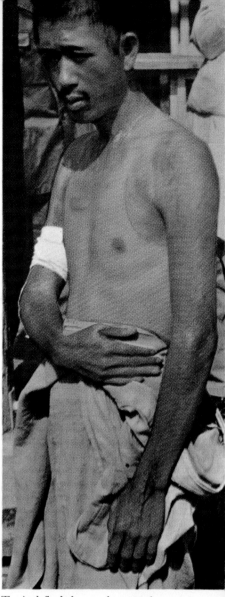

Typical flash burn of exposed portions of the skin as it appeared sixty-three days after the Nagasaki explosion. This is an instance in which exposed areas of a patient's body were burned while those covered by white or light-colored clothing—in this case a light-weight singlet—were protected from the infrared radiation.

appearance the blood proteins measured by the copper sulfate method were only 4.6 gm/100cc.

We had a most interesting time and obtained valuable data. Returned late to assist after dinner with the records. During the evening we subdivided the students and junior members into teams, each under a senior Japanese physician, so that the survey work which is to start tomorrow hopefully will go smoothly. Attention was paid to known evidences of compatibility.

October 24: Three survey groups were arranged as follows: to Yokogowa, Team 1 (Dr. Ishikawa) and Team 2 (Dr. Kitamoto) with Captain Rosenbaum; to Onaga, Team 3 (Dr. Yasuda) with Dr. Koch; to Kannon, Team 4 (Dr. Ito) and Team 5 (Dr. Hatano) with Major Kramer. The plan was for the younger doctors and students to be checked by the senior physicians in charge of the teams and by the Americans, who also participated actively in the work. Each team took its laboratory equipment for performing blood counts on every fifth patient. Our sergeants acted as drivers and performed laboratory work as required. On returning, all teams reported remarkable cooperation from the police and the people. All records were completed and checked by 11:00 P.M.

October 26–30: During these days the survey work progressed apace and the teams seemed congenial, but the work was hard and of a routine nature. Fortunately the weather, although cold, was clear most of the time, and there was no undue hardship for the waiting patients. Attempts to stagger the clinic visits met with only modest success, and most of the patients were on hand in the morning when the group arrived. Some stood patiently for several hours before they could be questioned, examined, and "treated" with vitamin pills.

At the same time old records of discharged patients from the major hospitals such as the Ujina, Red Cross, Prefectural, and Niho, and autopsy protocols, were being transcribed at Ujina or in the several institutions. All members were rotated through this work so that there would be a change from the daily grind of the survey. A remarkable body of information was being accumulated. However, patients with only minor injuries who had died, presumably from radiation effect, were not well-represented. Some records of such patients were said to be at Iwakuni Naval Hospital. We therefore

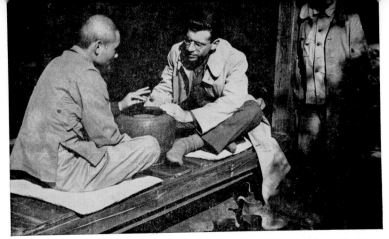

Lieut. J. Philip Loge having a conversation with a patient during a follow-up visit at the patient's farm on October 23, 1945. The patient was a soldier who suffered severe radiation effect. At the time of the follow-up visit he was regaining his hair and was able to work.

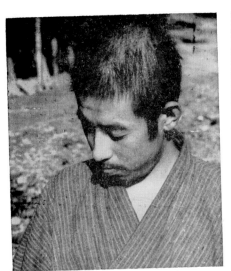
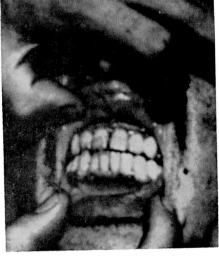

Left: Another patient, O——, visited on October 23. He had been hospitalized at Ujina for severe radiation illness. At the time the photograph was taken his hair had grown back almost completely.

Right: The same patient, with almost completely healed hemorrhagic and ulcerated lesions of the gums. He permitted a spinous process puncture to be performed at this time.

planned to visit this institution. Also, autopsies of persons who died in the first few days, which had been performed by Major Yamashina or by Dr. Sugiyama of Kyoto University (there were conflicting reports) were also to be obtained. During the past several weeks Dr. Tsuzuki and the Japanese majors have been preparing a consolidated list of institutions outside of Hiroshima to which people had been evacuated and which are to be visited before concluding the work in Japan.

Our master distribution chart of the patient survey was growing. Specifications as to source of the subjects for the survey were altered to provide good representation from the various sectors by appropriate instructions to the police officers. These were amazingly successful. The list of suffixes to indicate the source of the patients also was growing. By the end of the work the number of suffixes was large, and they are reproduced here to provide some idea of the scope of the investigation:

Aj	— Ajina
C	— City Hall
E	— Eba Branch of the First Army Hospital
F	— Funakoshi
Fk	— Fukuyama Army Hospital
G	— Gion-Nagatsuka
H	— Hiroshima High School
Hr	— Hiroshima Railroad Station
I	— Iwakuni
J	— Prefectural Hospital (at Kusatsu)
Kg	— Kramer Girls School
Ki	— Kaitaichi
Ko	— Koimachi
Ku	— Kaijin-Kai (Kure)
M	— Mitsubishi Hospital
N	— Niho
On	— Onaga
Ot	— Otake
Ou	— Ouzu
P	— Post Office Hospital
Pe	— Early Post Office cases
Pr	— Prison
R	— Red Cross Hospital (Hiroshima)

S	— Saijyo
Sa	— Second Army Hospital
U	— Ujina Hospital
Uh	— Ushida
Uj	— Ujina Public School No. 1
Us	— Ujina Public School No. 2
Ya	— Yaga
Yo	— Yokogawa
Ono	— Ono Hospital
Ush	— Ushida Hospital (Kyoto Research Committee patients)
Kps	— Kyoto Prefectural Medical School (cases studied at Kyoto)
Kps-H	— Kyoto Prefectural Medical School (cases studied at Hiroshima)
Tot	— Tottori Army Hospital
Takatsuke	— Takatsuke Branch of the Osaka Medical Faculty
Osk	— Osaka Medical School
Kyoto	— Kyoto University
Kobe	— Kobe University
Okayama	— Okayama Medical School
Om	— Okayama Military Hospital

October 30, 1945: In the afternoon Comdr. Shields Warren arrived, together with his party and Colonel DeCoursey. Commander Warren was an old friend from pre-war days and a fellow member of the Interurban Pathology Society. He told me that he had naturally joined in the investigation with Colonel Oughterson, as a friend from Scotty's Boston days, since his own team was small and consisted of a translator and of several Navy officers and enlisted men. They were now living and working as one with the Nagasaki unit. It had been decided to include the Navy group in the Joint Commission and to produce a common report.

[Dr. Warren was well prepared for the atomic bomb casualty study, since he was the author of a number of articles in the *Archives of Pathology* on radiation effect. These had been collected into a monograph. After the war, Dr. Warren was director of the Division of Biology and Medicine of the U.S. Atomic Energy Commission from 1947 to 1952.]

Today occurred the only unpleasant incident with the Japanese until now. Major Sinclair, the language officer for the Nagasaki group, was wandering through the buildings, and in going through the kitchen he had addressed some remarks to one of the men working there. The man apparently failed to understand Sinclair's Japanese. Sinclair thought him rude and slapped him across the face in a manner that he thought appropriate to Japanese custom. This caused a minor furor and great embarrassment. Things are currently tense, but we have our people to smooth things over.

October 31: Took Colonel Oughterson and Nagasaki guests on what we have now laid out as the "grand tour." This includes all of the fascinating evidences of blast and heat damage in the shrine area at the Chugoku Army headquarters, the "Korean Building" with the shadowing on the concrete there, and the remarkable view of the Commercial Museum and the area of the hypocenter. All were fascinated by the outlines of men and vehicles on the Bantai Bridge. At another bridge farther from the hypocenter, Scotty found a charred pole with the light shadow of leaves of a castor bean plant. The plant had grown anew.

In the evening we discuss the total magnitude of the work. Scotty suggests that "more than 5,000 cases must be studied." This seems a staggering load to those who are laboring daily at the task of seeing the patients, doing the laboratory work, and transcribing the detailed records, often until midnight or later. Our teams have, however, admittedly become highly efficient, and we can survey as many as 300 patients each day, the students doing most of the history-taking and requiring less and less supervision. I stress the desire of everyone to complete the job and to get home without delay and point out that morale will be difficult to maintain under the load if a definite goal is not set. Scotty has to hurry off by train to Tokyo. Later discussion with the junior members does indeed elicit grumbling. Remarks are made about "AWOL Oughterson" and Jack Rosenbaum spends the rest of the evening composing a song to the tune of "Get Me One Thousand Roses":

> Get me ten thousand cases,
> Wipe those smiles off your faces
> And stay out here another year,

While Doctor Tsuzuki
Who's my favorite cookie
Gives you all a loud Bronx cheer.

There may be other surveys later,
Kinda think they'd be fun!
Tsuzuk' and I will plan them—
At the Club 21.

So get me ten thousand cases,
Forget other places.
Hiroshima is now your home!

To bed very late and very tired.

November 1: In the early morning with Dr. Nakao received patients from the Ujina out-patient clinic itself. One of the most striking was patient Shigemori, a former soldier in the Nakao group who had many signs of radiation effect. There was marked epilation. Hemorrhages and gum lesions were fading, but the latter were not quite healed and peridontal ulcerations were still present. A second bone marrow was obtained by Dr. Nakao using the spinous-process technique.

Drove to Gion with Dr. Mitani in the afternoon, where arrangements were easily made with the senior police officer. It is remarkable that the police control of the population is still firm. To obtain any given number of persons from any particular locality it has only been necessary to speak to the police chief, who obtains precisely what is requested at precisely the right time. The people who appear have been entirely docile, submit readily to questioning and examination, and seem grateful for the vitamin pills which are doled out after the examination.

The chief showed us a very handsome sword that had been turned in in accordance with a U.S. occupation order. It had been previously viewed by Colonel Mason and was reserved for him. A charming Nisei interpreter, Jean Ito, assisted in the demonstration. Later in the afternoon proceeded similarly to Koi to arrange work for the coming Saturday morning.

Late in the evening discussed with Colonel Mason our food problem. The thirty cases of Ten-in-One rations that had been obtained were supposed to be sufficient for sixty men for forty days. Numerous guests, both American and Japanese, had made considerable inroads, and our supply was running low. Colonel Mason had cheerfully assumed the role of supply and senior contact officer, and promised to relieve our looming shortage with additional supplies from the Kure depot.

Thursday, November 2: This was a lovely bright and clear morning. Colonel DeCoursey and Commander Warren were ready to return to Nagasaki. We bade them a fond good-by. Dr. Ishii in the last few days had been busily translating the Japanese protocols by himself into German, since I was thoroughly occupied with visitors and with trips into the surrounding communities to facilitate survey work through the police. The protocols were then ready for dictation in English to Sergeant Huffaker. We completed the identification and separation of all of the old protocols, and prepared a consolidated list by transcribing all of the essential information onto the front sheets. The day was ideal for photography. In the afternoon rode with Colonel Mason to the city and photographed many of the buildings in the region of the hypocenter and also obtained panoramic views from the top of the "Korean Building."

In the evening, continued with the transcription of the records. Everyone was in better spirits, in keeping with the weather.

November 3: Beautiful weather persists. Dr. Ishii and I took advantage of it to photograph the remaining gross material. The alcohol was successful in restoring a semblance of the previous color. Our clinical teams in the field with Ishii then plunged into the task of completing the translation of the autopsy protocols. In the early evening we continued with the protocols of three of the earliest patients who had died within the first few days at Iwakuni. The stress under which these patients were treated and the haste with which the autopsies had to be performed was reflected in the sketchiness of the records. The tissues of these patients, however, were not yet available for study, but must represent some of the most important material. Ishii's quality and worth are daily becoming more apparent. He has become a firm and helpful friend. His education in pathology is superb. He is modest, eager to learn, and willing to listen. He is also, like most of his countrymen who are with us, absolutely tireless. He voices real enthusiasm for completing the work and we continue into the small hours, until all protocols in hand are finished.

November 3: The strain is beginning to tell, and everyone is now tired. Major Kramer came back late from Gion with his group and was full of disgust and complaints because of difficulties in dealing with the huge mass of patients.

We had been collecting clothing that had been damaged during the explosion, and the brilliant sunshine was ideal for photography. Many garments had been brought in that showed the effects of differential heat absorption during the flash. The darker portions of the pattern were completely burned out and the lighter portions spared. Where the heat had struck more directly, burning was more complete, but where the incidence of the rays was oblique there was only partial scorching resulting from small differences in color and other factors determining absorption of heat. We used color film and obtained many close-ups with a portrait lens.

Discussed with Japanese colleagues the possibility of a holiday for tomorrow, which is Sunday. Major Motohashi came forward with a proposal for a picnic and mushroom hunt which was joyfully accepted by all. The actual occasion of the meeting was the report just completed by Major Motohashi of a most valuable casualty survey that had been conducted by him, Major Misono, and Drs. Miyazaki and Nakatoni. This was based on the principle that we had earlier discussed of identifying groups of persons at known distances from the hypocenter and under known conditions of protection. The school children were an excellent group for this investigation since their fate had later been determined by responsible authorities as the municipal offices of the city were reestablished. Some of the data had been collected by the principals. The headmaster of a private school, Rio Yasuda, had submitted a detailed separate report. He presented a table of mortality and injuries that could be correlated with the actual distance of the school buildings. Most of these were of a standard two-story Japanese wood-and-tile construction, rather similar to the barracks buildings in which we were living and working at Ujina. Some of the children had not been in the schools, but were in the open firebreaks. They were exposed to flash burns and, if close enough, to radiation, while those in school were exposed to only the latter. The table classified the groups according to position and whether known dead, missing (presumed

A view from the roof of the Businessmen's Club. The shrine area bordering the military encampment is at the lower margin. It is pitted with foxholes. The broad avenue at the southern margin of the encampment is shown, and in the far distance the tall Fukuya department store is seen. A street car is visible.

A view toward the northeast from the Businessmen's Club. Across the military encampment is the moated region of the castle. In this area are the remains of the Chugoku army headquarters, seen as a low white building. To the right and just above the center of the photograph is the large dark Communications Department Building.

dead), untraced (no information available), injured, or alive and well. I congratulated Major Motohashi, since this is the most important accomplishment in obtaining protection data to the present time.

Everybody's spirits are lifted as we work late into the night transcribing the records of the day's surveys.

Sunday, November 4: A beautiful day dawned for the picnic and mushroom (*matsutake*) hunt, which is traditional at this time of year. Colonel Mason and I and as many as could fit rode in a jeep through the lovely clear morning to the hillside that had been selected. This was on Ushidayama to the northeast. All of the land was owned by three men. Permission was obtained by Major Motohashi, who led the party up the hill winding through the elevated pathways on the ridges alongside the rice paddies, now ready for harvesting. We ascended to the tall pines above the terraced paddies. At one level all of the trees facing the city were scorched brown, but their protected sides still retained traces of greenery. This represented the flash burn on the vegetation that occurred at the moment of the explosion. As we went higher we could see the terrain below that had been devastated all around the Higashi drill field. Against the flat background could be seen the framework of a concrete building that had crumpled away from the hypocenter, showing clearly the direction of blast impact. The dark green of the post office building was also visible above the plain. We are told that it was an annual custom dating back to feudal times for the lords to permit the peasants and villagers to go on the mushroom hunt at this time of year; we are merely following tradition. The mushrooms are found among the roots of the pine trees in moist, sweet-smelling soil, and are well-hidden. There are shouts whenever a fine specimen is discovered. The *matsutake* are large, white, and succulent. All are said to be safe to eat. A very fine tramp of some four or five hours is enjoyed by everyone. Friendships glow; national differences are forgotten; the horrors of the war and the intensity and strain of the work are far below and behind. The mushrooms are brought down to the edge of a paddy. Here is the still green tree line, where they are roasted under the soughing pine boughs in a shallow pit in small pans. They are marvelous with soy sauce containing a fair amount of sugar. The rice is cooked in a very large pot. We are so hungry that it is not quite done when we try the first bowls. Colonel Mason and I discuss ways and means of obtaining additional rice rations for the group, hoping that our previous inroads will not have been taken too seriously by our own government authorities. Then home to a hot bath in the communal Japanese style. Then, still glowing, we all go back to the records to get everything up to the moment and to plan for future operations.

November 5: Revivified, everyone was smiling and actually eager to plunge into the work this morning. Went early to Niho, where we met a Japanese, Mr. Ninon, who had been in Hawaii for forty years. He had a beautiful chrysanthemum garden which made a great hit with Colonel Mason. The village was relatively intact. It had narrow streets lined by the Japanese houses which had a weathered beauty. Dr. Mason found a shop where he bought some silk. Later we drove to Ushida, where again arrangements were made with the local police officer for a survey to follow, and then to Yokogowa. The police station there was another center for collecting Japanese weapons, and we went in hope of obtaining a sword. None were as yet available. Colonel Mason, however, found in the village a handsome pair of lacquer *getta*, the wooden shoes worn by *geisha*. Dr. Mason is quite good at haggling, and the purchase was made after a pleasant delay. We then continued back to Hiroshima to see the director of the Red Cross Hospital, Dr. Takeuchi, who was glad to let us begin a clinic in this hospital designed to start on November 10. In the afternoon we went to see the vice mayor, Mr. Morishita, whom we had contacted to supply figures on the distribution of the population within the city. The information was not yet available.

Then to Kure in the hunt for much-needed supplies. Met Lieutenant Colonel Jenkins, who introduced us to Major Winslow, in charge of the Twenty-sixth Medical Laboratory. He supplied us with some paraffin, and methyl alcohol for our Wright's stain. Inspected the facilities of the laboratory, which was now functioning. Then finally home. A letter had been received in the meantime from Colonel Oughterson from Tokyo, stating that he had consulted statisticians, who had advised that 5,000 cases would not be enough, when distributed among the various sectors, to obtain accurate information on the symmetry or asymmetry of the atomic bomb effects. He also suggested, somewhat peevishly, that we were free to leave if we wanted to.

November 6: Early in the morning went to consult the authorities at the railroad office and there made arrangements for testing all of the employees of the road who were in the building, 4.6 kilometers away from the center. They provided a map of the city showing the burned-out areas. In the early afternoon again visited Mr. Morishita, the vice mayor, who allowed us to trace the fire map more accurately. The mayor also had promised some pictures of the city before the bombing which were to be ready on Saturday at 1:30 P.M.

Later in the afternoon drove to Otake. The chief of police was more than cordial, promised much cooperation, and said that the townspeople wished very much to be examined. He also promised three Japanese swords for our group. A friendly gift was in order, and a package of cigarettes was gratefully received. Then a long, cold ride home.

[We had been especially interested in performing a detailed survey at Otake, since this village, together with several nearby communities, was the home of a number of work parties who were at precisely known locations in Hiroshima at the moment of the explosion. These people returned to the village and were then carefully followed to recovery or death. This was one of the most valuable medical investigations in terms of providing accurate information on the effects of both burns and radiation, and on the calamitous consequences of a combination of the two.]

November 7: Expected to spend a quiet day of work at the laboratory, but found that a large team representing the U.S. Strategic Bombing Survey has arrived. With them as medical officer is Maj. Luther L. Terry of the U.S. Public Health Service, accompanied by a photographer. He is desirous of making a report on medical effects but has only a few days and no help except a photographer. He requests cooperation for preparation of a summary and help in obtaining photographs of patients. Since time is short we make a quick change in plans and take Major Terry and the photographer to the Post Office Hospital, where they make a number of photographs of patients familiar to us. We then return to Ujina and do the same

The title page of the original report of the Yasuda Girls' School prepared by the principal, Mr. R. Yasuda. (Microfilm.)

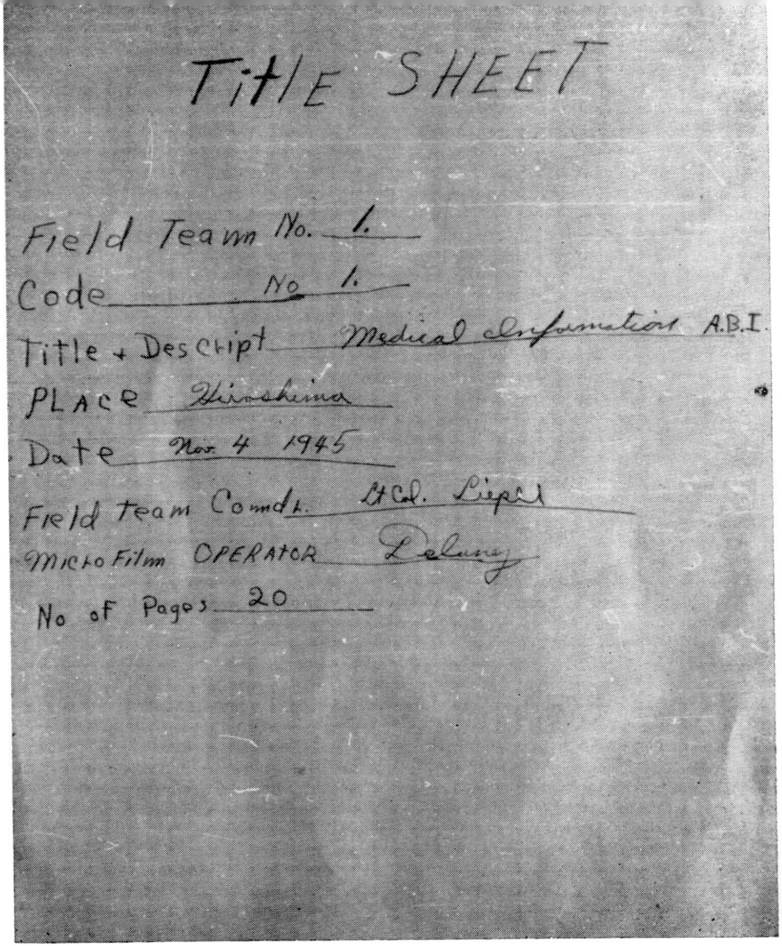

Title SHEET

Field Team No. 1.

Code No 1.

Title + Descript Medical Information A.B.I.

PLACE Hiroshima

Date Nov. 4 1945

Field team Comdt. Lt Col. Liepel

Micro Film OPERATOR Delaney

No of Pages 20

一、学徒出動者ノ工場及疎開地作業出動者遭難

調ノ中ニ包含セラル

二、職員遭難状況

会監 大谷 書類倒壊ニテ頭部裂傷及全身各所

ニ打撲傷ヲ受ク

事務員 田中某 無傷ニテ脱出シ会監ヲ助ケテ重要書類ノ

搬出及属品等ノ看護ニ当ル

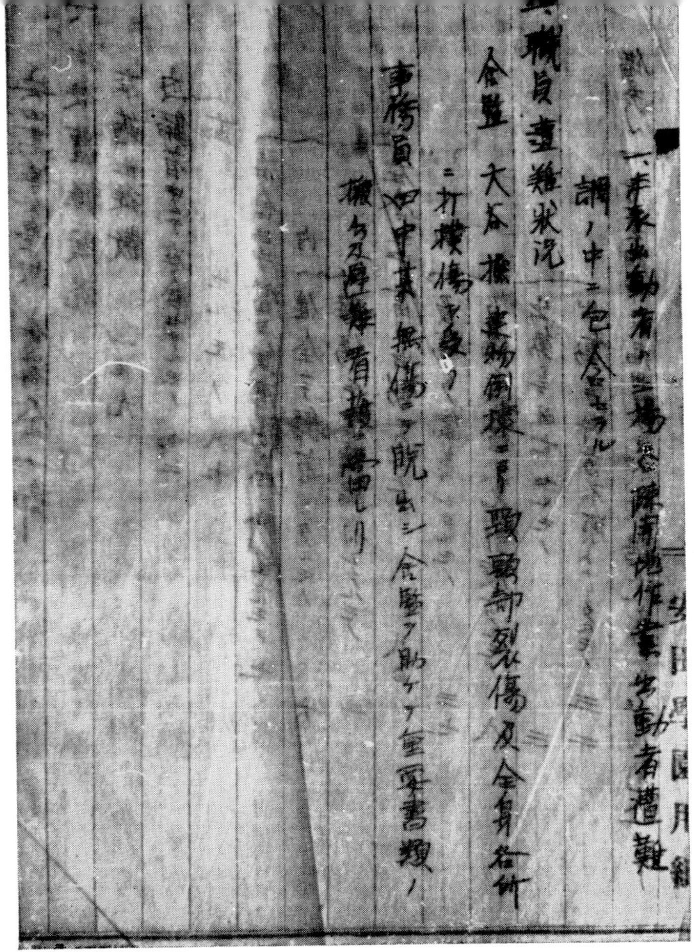

for in-patients. Major Terry also visits our team while it is in full swing at the Railroad Workers' Clinic. I proceed with transcriptions since we are falling behind. We are planning to start work at Otake early the following morning, and pray for good weather. Late in the afternoon a batch of mail is brought by a team of photographers who are actually assigned to us with Capt. Charles Brownell at their head. Their arrival and the mail instantaneously improve morale and we continue at our tasks until a very late hour.

[Dr. Luther L. Terry was a regular officer in the U.S. Public Health Service and rose to the rank of surgeon general in the early sixties. The negatives that were prepared at the time of his visit, which he mentions in an appreciative letter, were ultimately made available to the Joint Commission in Washington.

Charles Brownell had been an employee of the Eastman Kodak Company and was a very skillful photographer with a splendid feel for photography of patients and biological specimens. Unfortunately, some of the color film that was available to him had been ruined, apparently on Okinawa during the great storm of mid-September, and the transparencies, when developed, were a hideous blue. Others were quite superb. Through his help, his company was able to enlarge 35-mm. color film which was in my possession so that it was useful for preparing larger transparencies and, ultimately, for color reproductions, as of the "shadows" on the Bantai Bridge. In particular, minute sections of the 35-mm. transparencies were enlarged with a remarkable degree of detail and fidelity of color, as, for example, the lesions of patient Okita, whose case record appears earlier in this diary, and the postmortem specimen of a heart, showing petechiae.]

November 8: The weather is lovely and we are all set to depart at 7:45 in a convoy of two ambulances and two jeeps. At Otake we proceed to the large local school. The mayor and Dr. Nagaoka, a prominent physician who had followed the patients, are there to greet us. A large room in the school is filled with more than 200 people, all kneeling and sitting on mats. Some 580 residents of the town had been in the vicinity of the Koi Bridge (2,400 meters) at the time of the explosion. They had gone there to assist in the creation of firebreaks, since bombing raids were expected. Many are marked

A mushroom hunt on Ushidayama, near Hiroshima.

The rice harvest near Hiroshima, 1945.

Tokyo
Nov. 23, 1945

Col. Oughterson or
Col. Mason
Sir,

I should like to express my appreciation for the sincere cooperation and kindly treatment afforded me on my trip to Hiroshima. It is reassuring to encounter such fine spirit and to see a medical team doing its work so smoothly & efficiently.

Further prints of the photographs taken of patients in the Hiroshima area are being submitted. I promised Lt. Col. Liebow that I would turn the negatives over to you as soon as we obtained prints. However, the red tape of USSBS demands that the negatives be kept in the files of the Survey. They will be filed in Wash. and may be obtained by you there after Jan. 7th. Should you encounter any difficulty do not hesitate to contact me through Headquarters of U.S. Public Health Service and I will get them for you. The photos have been labeled on the back with the

key number for which you have further identification.
Again many thanks for your kindness to me while I was in Hiroshima —

Sincerely —

Luther L. Terry
Med. Division, USSBS.

A note of appreciation from Dr. Luther L. Terry, then a major in the U.S. Public Health Service. Dr. Terry later became surgeon general of the Public Health Service.

A group photograph taken during a visit to Iwakuni. The naval captain in charge is seated in front. Members of the Joint Commission are (right to left in the rear), Drs. Ishii and Kitamoto, in civilian dress. Capt. J. D. Rosenbaum is fourth from the right.

A clinic in session in a temporary building at the Hiroshima Central Railway Office at Ujina, November 7, 1945. Senior students and medical graduates are interviewing and examining survivors. Standing at the rear against the window is Dr. Luther L. Terry of the USSBS. Seated to his right is Major Kramer, and to his left is Dr. Hatano.

with the dark nut-brown pigmentation that we have come to call the mask of Hiroshima. Their faces were exposed in the open while facing the source of the explosion but not so close as to suffer actual third-degree burns, with loss of skin. The appearance is that of very deep sunburn, but the deep brown color has persisted for over three months. Other burns are of various shades of red and brown. The sight is horrible, since it involves some of the youngest and prettiest of the women.

These people made a remarkable contrast study to those of two other groups from Otake that were closer to the center of the city and that suffered from radiation effects that the people on the Koi Bridge were spared, despite the persistent widespread injury so easily visible. Dr. Nagaoka provided detailed information from his records, and the surviving foremen of the various groups were interviewed. We are graciously treated. At lunch had a large plate of rice and other assorted foods. By the end of the afternoon our group had interviewed 320 patients and had done a sampling study of laboratory data. At the end of the afternoon black tea and tangerines were served, and then another long, cold ride home. During this day acquired the three beautiful swords which had been promised by the police chief, one of which I presented to Calvin Koch. Then more transcriptions of records. Good talk with Major Terry, Captain Brownell, and the rest. Major Terry has been chilled, and we provide him with my sleeping bag for a more comfortable night. Our several large rooms are now well populated with sleepers.

[The detailed record of the experience of the "patriotic workmen's groups" from Otake and surrounding communities is one of the most interesting and revealing facets of our entire experience in Hiroshima. It was made especially vivid to us by the opportunity of examining the survivors en masse and of appreciating their remarkable spirit. It was possible to reconstruct the scene at the time of injury almost precisely. Through the interest of an observant and devoted physician of Otake, Dr. Nagaoka, accurate follow-up information was obtained in the quiet of the villages, away from the confusion of the aid stations and hospitals.

There were three major groups from Otake, each under the charge of a foreman who came to work in Hiroshima on the day of the bombing. The first, consisting of 580 persons under Mr. Hino, was crossing or had just crossed the Koi Bridge, approximately one-and-a-half miles from the hypocenter. These were predominantly the people seen in the clinic on November 8. Two men were killed by a collapsing building, and seven persons died within a week as the result of burns, but the others survived without signs of radiation effect.

The other groups had already arrived in the city and were awaiting assignment near the Otake Group Office, only 1,000 meters from the hypocenter. A reconstruction of the scene was possible from pre-strike stereoscopic air views of Hiroshima made by American reconnaissance planes. This was first accomplished by Lieutenant Elder during the visit of the British mission, and again at the request of the Joint Commission, at greater leisure, after returning to Washington, by Maj. A. L. Ganung, who also drew in the shadows as they would have been cast by the buildings in the glare of the bomb.

Men of Mr. Nagato's group had been lolling about in the shadows of the buildings prior to muster. Those in this group who were otherwise unhurt returned to Otake on foot. All subsequently showed evidence of radiation effect, with loss of hair, and most had petechiae. Seventy-two of 130 died of radiation effects, the first on August 20 and almost all the rest by September 13. The consequences were similar in the case of Mr. Morimoto's group, similarly shielded and only a short distance from the Nagato group.

Those who were on the bank of the river near the Temma Bridge, however, including groups from Kuba and Tachido villages and from the Ogata district, were unprotected from heat by the houses and suffered tremendous mortality, many on the spot and most by August 10. There were only 10 survivors of a total of 193 men, and these all showed radiation effect, even though their burns had partly healed.

This study provided a sharp contrast between those who had suffered purely from severe radiation effect at 1,000 meters and those who had, at the same distance, also been exposed to burns. The radiation complicated the effects of the burns, which in themselves were severe. The third group at 2,400 meters, without radiation effects, and with less severe burns, had a much higher survival rate.]

November 9: In the morning, began the photography work with Captain Brownell and his very pleasant crew. A permanent rack was made for the camera, and the equipment was prepared for synchro-

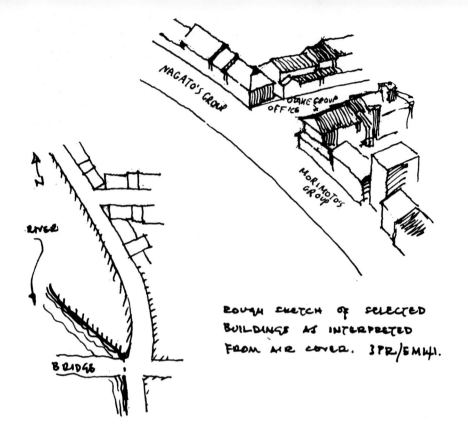

NAGATO'S GROUP

OTAKE GROUP
OFFICE

MORIMOTO'S GROUP

N

RIVER

BRIDGE

ROUGH SKETCH OF SELECTED
BUILDINGS AS INTERPRETED
FROM AIR COVER. 3PR/5M441.

21. November 1945

for Lt Cd Liebow,

Hiroshima Hospital;

compliments of the British Mission

A sketch prepared by Lieutenant Elder of the British mission, showing
the positions of the various Otake workmen's groups. The sketches of
buildings are based on an interpretation of stereoscopic pre-strike photographs made from a reconnaissance plane. There are slight differences
between this sketch and Major Ganung's interpretation. (The sketch is
dated November 21, 1945.)

A chart showing the positions of the Otake workmen's groups and of the Koi bridge. People in the Hino group on the Koi Bridge suffered chiefly from burns, but not from radiation effect.

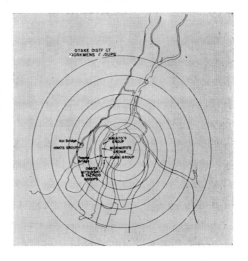

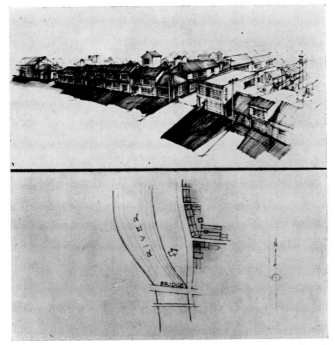

A reproduction of the perspective drawing prepared by Major Ganung from pre-strike air views, showing the shadows of the buildings as they would have appeared in the glare of the bomb. Those groups that were in the shadows of the buildings—the Nagato group to the left of the roadway and the Morimoto group to the right—suffered radiation effect. Those that were on the riverbank near the Temma Bridge, shown below (groups from Kuba, Tachido, and Ogata), had a tremendous mortality rate from burns complicated by radiation injury.

A view of the Koi Bridge, 2,400 meters from the hypocenter. Members of the group from Otake were on or had just left this bridge at the time of the bombing.

The riverbank near the Temma Bridge (1,000 meters), which is shown in the background.

nized flash shots. This took a good part of the morning. Early in the afternoon, spent much time going over our records and observations to date with Dr. Terry, who was about to depart. He wished to take the negatives with him. I was fearful that they might be lost. He promised to give them to Colonel Schwichtenberg, now the senior medical officer at Advanced Headquarters in Tokyo. It is rumored that Colonel Dieuaide and General Morgan from the surgeon general's office, and Colonel Shull, the medical consultant of the Sixth Army, are to arrive in Hiroshima. Later in the evening was at work when the announcement came that Colonel Shull had indeed arrived. We welcomed him but had to plunge back to get the day's transcription work finished. Our first print was developed by Captain Brownell and his staff during the evening. The black-and-white work was superb.

November 10, 1945, Saturday: Early in the morning, continued with photography, chiefly of the specimens of clothing and autopsy material, with Captain Brownell's equipment. There is no certainty that my own 35-mm. shots will prove to be properly exposed, since I had no exposure meter when the photography was first done. Three items of clothing that had been brought in were especially remarkable. One was a girl's shirt with a pattern of small roses on the sleeves, shoulders, collar, and pocket flaps. Some of the roses had become completely burned through on the side most directly facing the explosion, but others on the curve of the sleeve showed brown scorching only of the darker petals of the roses, with the green of the leaves intact. The light pink background also was spared. Another shirt had a pattern of dark-blue polka dots against a lighter blue-green cloth. This showed similar effects, with less burning where the rays were more oblique. The third shirt consisted of striped rayon. In parts of it only certain folds had apparently been exposed to the flash, and here the dark stripes had disintegrated, leaving the white intact. We also photographed in black and white a piece of rice paper on which the brushed Japanese characters had been sharply burned out, although the rest of the paper was intact. This was from a schoolroom about one-and-a-half miles from the hypocenter.

[These clothes caused me some difficulty, since I carried them in my hand luggage on the way back to the United States. The luggage

The differential effect of dark and light surfaces in absorbing heat. The material is rice paper, used for a teacher's name card which was on the outside of a classroom facing the hypocenter at 2,300 meters. The inked characters, which say "Arai House," have been burned out, whereas the white paper has reflected the heat and is almost intact.

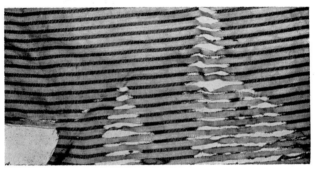

Scorching of the darker blue-black stripes on a garment, with less effect on the lighter stripes, by heat rays at 1,700 meters. Only certain folds of the garment on the side away from the bomb were in the path of the rays. On the near side, a portion of the cloth was charred. The patient suffered second- and third-degree burns of the chest, underlying the charred cloth where it was tightly stretched over the skin, and also of the exposed face, chest, arms, and neck.

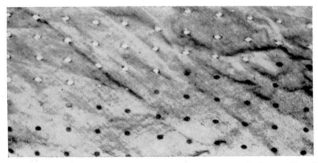

Charring and scorching of the dark blue portions of the polka dot pattern of a piece of clothing at 1,600 meters, with minimal effect on the lighter background. Some of the polka dots have been completely burned through; others are partially scorched.

was subject to inspection by customs in Hawaii, and the none-too-clean ladies' garments caused some eyebrows to be raised. This clothing was put on permanent display at the AFIP along with the records, specimens, and other materials, but unfortunately has become faded with the years.]

Then off with Dr. Mitani to Hiroshima Prison to arrange for a survey team visit. We thought this would provide an opportunity for investigating effects of the heat flash on men whose exact position was known and who (at 2,300+ meters) were beyond the range of severe gamma radiation. We had been told that some had been exercising in the open and others had been confined to their cells. A good comparison could be made of the effects of radiant heat on persons in the open and under various degrees of shading. Comparison with the Otake group that had been on the Koi Bridge in another part of the city at about the same distance from the hypocenter would also be of interest. We met the prison doctor, to whom we explained the aims of the survey, especially our need to know just where each man was—if near a window, whether it was open or not; the precise clothing; etc. Dr. Mitani also asked permission to perform some sperm counts on the prisoners, who would serve as controls for a study Dr. Okoshi was performing on persons exposed to radiation in Hiroshima. At the distance of the prison no significant radiation effect would be expected. Small gifts would be furnished those prisoners who cooperated. The prison medical officer was entirely agreeable to all of the proposals. Arrangements were made to begin the survey on Monday morning. We were introduced to the warden, who presented Dr. Mitani with a large basket of fine tangerines.

Later in the afternoon went again to the office of the vice mayor, who had kept his promise and left us a good collection of pictures from the various school books, postcards, etc., showing the city as it had been before the bombing. Later, more photography. Then a satisfying Japanese bath, some cribbage with Major Kramer, more work on records, and then to bed.

November 11, 1945: Early on this Sunday morning, went again to Otake with Dr. Ishii, who said that we had received an invitation to dine but was rather mysterious about it. It was a beautiful morning after a somewhat misty sunrise. We called first at the home of the

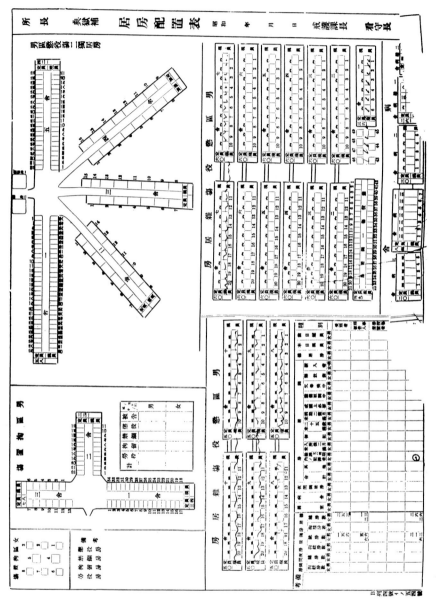

A plan of the cell blocks supplied by the chief warden at Hiroshima Prison, where a detailed study of burn injuries was performed by the Joint Commission. At 2,300 meters from the hypocenter, there were no serious immediate radiation injuries.

Notes made by Colonel Mason during an interview with the assistant warden of Hiroshima Prison. In the margin are doodlings simulating Japanese.

mayor and found that he had arranged for us to visit Dr. Nagaoka. We were escorted to the doctor's home. This was typically walled off from the street and had its own private court complete with dwarf trees. He was a rather tall middle-aged man with a lined, grave face and quiet demeanor, dressed in the traditional dark kimono. We were introduced to Mrs. Nagaoka. The reception was ceremonious and most gracious. *Sukiyaki* was served in the true Japanese manner with a charcoal stove in the middle of the table. Taro and *matsutake* were thrown in, together with small quantities of meat and chicken and much soy sauce and coarse brown sugar. The lady of the house did not partake of the meal, but appeared only occasionally to serve. Our conversation was entirely through interpreters, but I was able to capture a sense of Dr. Nagaoka's concern for the citizens of his village, many of whom had been his patients in the past. Most interesting was his evident appreciation of the scientific value of the records he had kept. After the fine dinner a beautiful blue silk *haori* (lady's short coat) was brought out and ceremoniously presented to me. Dr. Nagaoka said that he had learned I was planning to marry and that he hoped that my wife would be happy with this gift.

On returning I found that Colonel Mason had opened an acipak and all the chocolate and other good things were placed above his bed ready to be distributed. This was done for all hands.

November 12: Spent the morning photographing the remainder of the autopsy specimens with Charlie Brownell. Was informed in the early afternoon that three technicians were to arrive from the 262nd Station Hospital. They did indeed arrive, accompanied by Major Achenard and Captain Pierce. This was a tangible result of Colonel Oughterson's efforts to strengthen our staff. Dr. Ishii reported that

Left: A typical profile burn. The patient, a seventeen-year old nurse at the Red Cross Hospital, was exposed at 1,700 meters. There is depigmentation, sharply outlined by pigmented tissue in a very narrow band, and a crusted exudate in the peri-aural region.

Right: A typical "mask" burn in a prisoner at Hiroshima Prison (2,300 meters). The pigmentation has a deep chocolate-brown color. The outlines are very sharp. The upper portion of the neck was shaded by the mandible. At this distance there were no burns beneath the clothing. A blue prison cap protected the skin of the forehead.

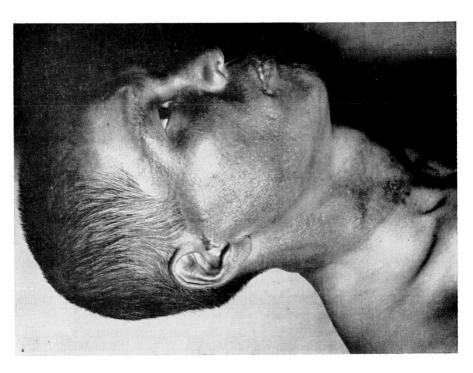

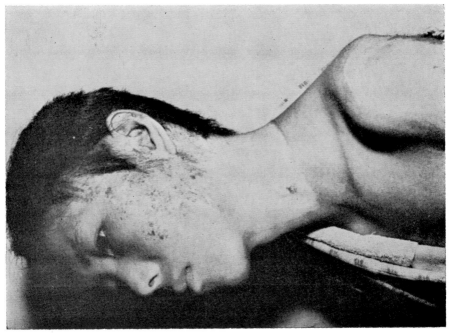

Hiroshima Castle before and after the bombing. Near the castle were the headquarters of the military forces in Hiroshima (800 meters).

Dr. Tamagawa of the Okayama University Medical School was in the city, and we went to meet him at the Post Office Hospital. He promised material, but had not as yet worked up the autopsies that he had performed in late August. We visited the morgue, which was in a shed behind the hospital, almost in the open air. Later in the cold afternoon, a fine bath, which this time had been reserved for the Japanese officers and physicians and for us. It was less gay than usual but also less crowded.

The teams that returned from the prison reported that the work was especially worthwhile. Colonel Mason had obtained a detailed record of casualties, with unusually complete follow-up data, since the survivors were still under imprisonment. In the evening, was assisted in translating captions and identifying details of the pictures that had been supplied by the mayor's assistant. We considered these a find because of photographic restrictions that had been in force in Hiroshima since the Manchurian war.

Dr. Murachi reported considerable progress in his major preoccupation with the building and protection studies, in which he was now assisted by Dr. Murai, an excellent radiologist from Tokyo who had joined the group. His investigations had identified tentatively a number of buildings suitable for obtaining the data desired: the Bankers' Club, the Nippon Bank, the Chugoku Electric Company Building, a large concrete underground shelter near Hiroshima Castle adjacent to the headquarters of the Chugoku Army, the Hiroshima broadcasting station (JOFK). All of these buildings were within 1,000 meters of the hypocenter. Drs. Murachi and Murai had begun the detailed work of inquiry and tracing of individual patients who had been at their desks or in other fixed positions. Since many of them were dead, Dr. Murachi said that it was a matter of going from one person to another in the various villages or on outskirts of the city to obtain hearsay reports, and confirmation when possible. This was difficult and time-consuming, but a surprising amount of useful information had already been gathered.

[At this time a less focused but still quite useful study was also in the making. This consisted of the compilation of reports on the fate of people in the major buildings, which made possible a comparison of the protective effect of concrete buildings as compared with wooden structures. For this purpose the report of the Communications Department, which had several buildings at various points in the city, was especially useful. Information on the fate of the personnel had been compiled by Dr. Hachiya. Similar information was obtained by questioning officials of the Hiroshima City Hall and Red Cross Hospital. In addition, since most of the school buildings had been of wood, the fate of the children in the buildings provided comparative data. Particularly useful was the report of the Yasuda Private School, which has been mentioned.]

November 13: Went to the Red Cross Hospital and took photographs of patients well known to us, one of a young nurse with depigmentation which was very severe, but outlined by a sharp line of dark brown.

Although the skies were gray and threatening, took the photographic team to Hiroshima Castle in the military headquarters area. The castle was a tangled pile of rubble on a stone base situated in a corner of a square plot of land surrounded by a moat. Photographed all aspects of the underground concrete bunker near the military headquarters, in which twenty young girls had served as telephone operators. Both inside and outside views were recorded. Dr. Murai had prepared a "shadow diagram" of the bunker. This showed the thickness of earth and concrete projected on the ground that would have intervened between a person in any part of the bunker and the gamma rays, assuming that they traveled in perfectly straight lines from the epicenter. We discussed the principles as they would apply to more complex structures, and it was quite clear that detailed building plans would have to be obtained. Despite the drizzle, visited several other underground shelters. In one, directly opposite the headquarters building, I found in the litter and rubble a blue-covered copy of *The Life of Clausewitz*, about the famous Prussian military tactician, written in English and extensively annotated in Japanese. The covers were faded and stained with moisture, but this treasure itself was essentially intact.

In the evening, was delighted to find that Dr. Nakao had acquired additional information, largely blood data, on the early patients in the Iwakuni series. These were transcribed. Ishii has had no success in obtaining additional autopsy material, but the search is still on.

November 14: In the early morning, photographed patients with Captain Brownell's team at the Post Office Hospital. At the same time, obtained tissues from many autopsy cases. Most of these seemed irrelevant or were lacking in material. Dr. Tamagawa seemed well informed but talked about each case at great length. Dr. Ishii was of the greatest help in abstracting the monologue.

Later in the afternoon had a most interesting visit at the prison, where inmates were photographed. Many had the same mask-like,

The exterior and interior of the communications bunker, Chugoku army headquarters (800 meters).

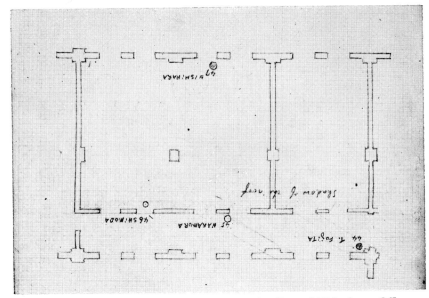

The initial sketch of the building plan of the Central Telephone Office, showing the positions of certain people who were subsequently traced.

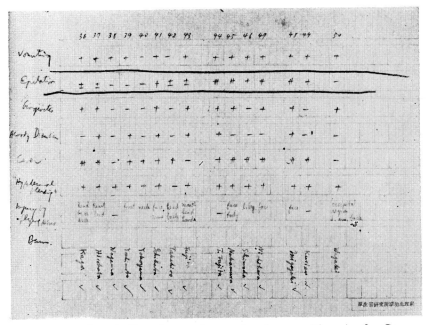

Notes regarding findings in certain people whose positions in the Central Telephone Office were known and for whom shielding data were calculated.

クラウゼヴヰッツ兵學要領

原書は The Reality of War: A Companion to Clausewitz と題す。「戰爭の實相」の義にて、「クラウゼヴヰッツの伴侶」とはかの著名なる獨逸將軍の大兵學書「大戰學理」の要を摘み、その研究の助に供するを云ふ。 著者はもと Gordon Highlanders とて目下第七十五步兵聯隊の稱ある隊に屬せし Major Stewart L. Murray である。 この書の Popular Edition は Captain A. Hillard Atteridge によりて編せらる。 編者には別に Famous Modern Battles, The British Army of To-day 等の著書がある。

此書には先づ編者の序文がある。 その中にオクスフォード大學の戰史敎授 Spenser Wilkinson の Clausewitz に關する評が載せてあるがそれはこゝに省く。

第一章はクラウゼヴヰッツ傳である、特に英人に告ぐるはじめの數行を省いて直ちに傳記のところから掲載する。

A portion of the first page of *The Life of Clausewitz*, from a bunker at the Japanese military headquarters near Hiroshima Castle.

The imprint of the Japanese army Transportation Corps on the flyleaf of the book.

deeply pigmented burns as the Otake patients. Some remarkable shadows on the wall of the prison cast by one wall against the wall at right angles to it were found by Captain Rosenbaum and photographed.

Dr. Okoshi had good success in obtaining semen specimens from the prisoners. On the preceding day Colonel Mason had brought along a supply of chocolate bars, which were used as a reward for the men who cooperated.

In the evening I was appalled to discover that some Iwakuni cases consisted of protocols that did not match autopsy materials or that there were tissues from some early deaths without protocols. Asked Dr. Ishii to visit Iwakuni to see that everything was properly lined up. He seemed embarrassed by this difficulty and assured me that everything would soon fall into line.

[The eager and excellent photographic team consisting of Capt. Charles G. Brownell, M.A.C., and Capt. Ted Bloodhart, S.C., which at long last had been assigned to us, was a most important and stimulating addition. Much of my time in those days was spent in bringing their talents to bear on the photography of tissue specimens, clothing, and patients who had become familiar in the various hospitals and clinics, or of new and worthy subjects as they were identified by the teams in the field. Later they performed yeoman service in recording the appearance of the effects of physical phenomena such as the "shadows" on the bridges and buildings. The major buildings and shelters in which the special casualty studies were being performed were also photographed. For correlative work, one set of views of the buildings was made from the direction of the hypocenter.]

November 15: Most of the day was spent with Brownell-Bloodhart, *et al.* making numerous photographs of the large buildings, mostly in the direction of the rays from the bomb for correlation with protection factors. All of the important rooms were photographed.

Upon returning, saw Zenker's solution being mixed and guessed at once that an autopsy was in the offing. There was indeed a case to do: a lung abscess. Dr. Ishii and I performed the autopsy together. The patient was a thirty-one-year-old soldier who had been recovering from radiation-induced aplastic anemia but who died on the hundredth day. This was the ultimate consequence, perhaps, of focal pulmonary necrosis which had developed during the earlier agranulocytosis from which the patient had suffered. During the autopsy I saw a number of persons in the hallway outside the small and none-too-clean autopsy room peering in whenever the door was opened. Among them I noted an elderly gentleman in street clothes, whom I assumed to be the undertaker. When I asked Dr. Ishii whether this was true, he inquired and then told me nonchalantly that it was the patient's father waiting to claim the body. I was distressed, but the elderly gentleman himself showed no emotion. After the autopsy was completed I found that the first photos of the specimen had returned. These were reasonably good but rather too full of highlights, and had to be redone. The remainder of the day was spent with Drs. Murachi and Murai in compiling the information that had been obtained to date on the building and shielding studies.

[At this time only the position in the buildings and fate of certain persons could be established, and a crude estimate made of the direction of the rays. The building plans needed to determine the relation to the airburst itself and thus the angle of incidence of the gamma rays, assuming a limited source, were not available. Immense labor was necessary to obtain the projections of all the components of the buildings, exclusive of the furnishings, in order to determine depth of shield, which was calculated in "water equivalent."]

November 16: The survey work is now nearly complete. Only Loge and Koch are involved with the teams, working at the Post Office Hospital clinic, which is still active. Here employees of the Communications Department are seen as out-patients.

Spent most of the day in the field with Drs. Murai and Rosenbaum and the photographic group at the radio station. This was a small, battered, dark-green concrete building. Parts of it seemed unsafe, and the work was conducted gingerly with tests to see whether the weight of a man could be borne. Although only a few persons were exposed in this building, their positions were accurately known, and Murachi had been insistent on the value of the detailed study. Also began photography on the Nippon Bank, a much larger and more complex structure in which there were only a few survivors. Its proximity to the hypocenter and its very heavy construction could provide valuable

The Bankers' Club (200 meters from the hypocenter).

Hiroshima City Hall. Despite its burned-out condition, this building was used to conduct the business of the city throughout the time the Joint Commission was at work in Hiroshima.

data on the amount of shielding necessary for protection. Returned to find Major Kramer in the midst of transcription of the Communications Bureau reports. These gave raw survival data for the employees, but not visitors, in the various divisions of the Communications Department. These comprised several large buildings in the heart of the city.

November 17: Continued with photographic documentation of buildings near the hypocenter with Kramer and Rosenbaum, whose clinical duties are now complete, and Murai, Murachi, and the photographers.

Colonel Oughterson finally arrived late in the evening, followed by Dr. Tsuzuki not long after. An impromptu meal was prepared and then, with Colonel Mason and Dr. Tsuzuki, talked into the small hours on the progress that had been made and what was still to be done. Scotty was particularly interested in the work with the Otake villagers and what had been learned from the survey of school children that had been carried out largely on the initiative of the Japanese medical officers. After looking at my now crowded distribution chart, Scotty agreed that although more patients would be better, the survey work could be considered at an end, and he would be satisfied with our total of well over 6,000 cases. This was to my immense relief, since I knew that those who had been doing the daily stint were weary and anxious to go home, or at least to have a change. There remained still many important collections of material elsewhere that had been gathered by various investigating groups from the Japanese institutions. Also, some patients had been evacuated in numbers to other places. Some of these institutions contained the particularly precious records of patients examined and investigated soon after the bombing. We had already collected some of the most valuable material in surveys at Iwakuni and at Saijyo Sanatorium. The latter required an overnight trip. There still remained a number of institutions in Okayama and in the Kyoto district, especially at the Imperial University there, and we still had the major problem of obtaining building plans from the central offices in Tokyo.

It was agreed that it would be best to send a team ahead to Kyoto to begin the transcription of records and review of collections of material there. Major Kramer would be in the advance party, and Colonel Mason and Captain Rosenbaum would join him there after

The Nippon Bank (250 meters) seen from the outside, with the camera in line with the hypocenter.

Outside the bank, eighteen inches of cinders had been placed on top of the tile to protect against fire raids. (Captain Brownell is in the photo.)

An interior view of the bank, showing a shattered concrete partition.

completing work at Hiroshima. My own assignment was to go to the intermediate points, allowing the most time for Okayama, as soon as the shielding and population surveys could be completed here.

The chief remaining problem, and perhaps one of the most important objectives of the Joint Commission, was to establish mortality and casualty curves, in order that information on particular groups— for example, those relatively protected in concrete buildings—could be related to the general casualties at the same distance from the hypocenter. Since it was now very late, we determined to postpone this discussion until tomorrow so that all could contribute their thoughts. This problem had never been far from our minds.

November 18: Much of the day was spent by the entire group in discussion of how best to obtain the information for constructing a casualty curve in relation to distance. The best idea put forward is that a sampling should be made of survivors who are to be questioned concerning not only their own injuries but also the fate of their relatives who were in the city. As we discuss the matter it is obvious that there will be some error, since certain persons may have been en route and some may not have been in the place where they were supposed to be. We decide to proceed with this, since it appears to be the only way in which we can obtain information regarding persons now dead. It is clear that we will need help from those more expert in population studies, especially in the matter of proper sampling. Colonel Oughterson suggests that such men must be available on the USSBS team, which has now left this area. He promises to investigate at once. Our Japanese colleagues also suggest that older school girls could perform this survey very well once the list of persons is selected.

In the late afternoon Dr. Tamagawa arrived, and we invited him to a late supper with us. He brought more records, and the transcriptions of these were begun, with both Tamagawa and Ishii at work.

November 19: Drs. Tsuzuki and Oughterson left for Nagasaki in the hope of obtaining expert help with the population study from the USSBS, now at work there. This morning, made a tour with Brownell and Co. to photograph the various "shadows." Most of these were still clearly visible but the penumbra effect on the "Korean Building" was less evident. Photographed Brownell himself actually standing in the footmarks on the Bantai Bridge.

Returned in time for a farewell dinner for Milton Kramer, who was leaving for Kyoto to begin the work of collecting case records and other materials available there. Arrangements had been made by Dr. Tsuzuki. Major Kramer left by train in company with Drs. Ito, Hatano, and Gotoh. We were to be reunited in Kyoto within the next two weeks.

The remainder of the afternoon was spent in histological work, cutting and staining, to bring our material closer to completion. To bed late at night.

November 20: Colonel Oughterson returned from Nagasaki. He had in the meantime contacted the USSBS in regard to help with the demography of the casualty study. A navy lieutenant, Mr. Nisselson, who is said to have a good statistical background, has been assigned to us and is to come soon. Later in the day, without our prior knowledge, members of a large British mission arrived with Colonel Solandt, a Canadian physiologist, in charge of the casualty aspects. They seemed a very keen and pleasant group. We made a working tour of the more interesting and revealing institutions and landmarks in midafternoon. More of the building exteriors were photographed by Brownell. On returning, discussed census figures with Colonel Solandt and found some discrepancies between his data and ours that must be resolved. Of major interest to the British group are the protection and survival data. We discuss our procedure and findings to date in great detail. They were, of course, fascinated by the Otake workmen's groups and the fact that good follow-up data are available. We discussed the possibility of making a visual reconstruction of the city before the bombing from air maps in order to establish the shadowing effects of the buildings, and they said they would attempt it.

November 21: We spent a part of the morning reviewing the medical findings and protection data with Colonel Solandt and others of his group. Later in the morning we returned to the mayor's office with Colonel Solandt and again had a long talk, stressing the necessity for correct data and also the need for the rice ration lists for setting up the population survival study. The city now is rather heavily populated with investigating groups concerned largely with estimates of damage. Lieutenants Martin and Montgomery are here from Survey

Team No. 4. On returning we meet Group Captain Thomas and Group Commander Bronowski of the British mission which has been busily at work on the stereoscopic pre-bombing air maps. Lieutenant Elder has prepared a perspective drawing of the banks of the river near the Koi Bridge, where the Otake workmen's groups were situated at the moment of the explosion. Actual buildings and the position of the men were identified with the help of our Japanese colleagues who had been with us at Otake.

Jack Rosenbaum left for Nagasaki in mid-afternoon. He had requested this trip before joining the group in Kyoto.

[For the casualty studies several basic pieces of information were required. The first of these was the actual population of the city on August 6. The best estimate that could be made, 255,000, was on the basis of the rice-rationing figures of June 30, 1945. Those, as of the last of July, had been lost in the fires of August 6. An estimate based on newspaper circulation gave a figure lower by 25,000, but this was considered minimal and less reliable because it was based on more assumptions than the estimate for the rationing data. Data on the distribution of the population in the various sectors were also requested from Mr. Morishita, the vice mayor, and he ultimately complied.

For the construction of the casualty curve, the method finally chosen after consultation with the statisticians, Lieut. H. Nisselson, USSBS, Lieut. M. Habel, F.A., and Dr. Motosaburo Masuyama, Institute of Statistical Mathematics, Tokyo Imperial University, was to secure a random sample of the population aged between thirteen and sixty. The first problem was to randomize the choice of precincts. For this purpose a designation number, 270, was chosen. The populations of the individual precincts were added, and the first selected was the one in which the cumulated population fell closest to 270. This number was then added to the new total, and the populations of the precincts were further cumulated, the one chosen being that which fell closest to the new total and so on. On this basis, 265 of the 523 available precincts were chosen. A national census had, fortunately, been taken early in November 1945. The Hiroshima High School girls were responsible for handing out and collecting a questionnaire, directed to each twentieth person on the census lists of the designated precincts, that was to provide information not only about the persons

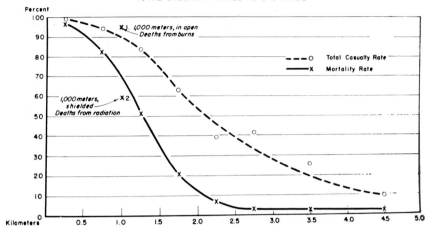

HIROSHIMA

RELATION OF MORTALITY AND
TOTAL CASUALTY RATES TO DISTANCE

1,000 meters, in open
Deaths from burns

Total Casualty Rate
Mortality Rate

1,000 meters,
shielded
Deaths from radiation

The general casualty and mortality curves in Hiroshima, as determined from the population study. Against the general curve are shown mortality figures from the two Otake groups, some of whom were shielded from burns, although not protected from radiation effect, by being in the shadow of Japanese houses, and some of whom were in the open on a riverbank and suffered both burns and radiation injury.

selected for the sample, but also about their relatives in the city. Some 3,740 of the cards issued to 4,700 persons in the sample were returned. This procedure was supervised by a group led by Lieut. (later Capt.) Marvin E. Habel and Dr. Masuyama, who also ultimately calculated the results. These cards, after exclusion of duplications, provided information on the fate of 20,586 people at various distances from the hypocenter. Confidence in the validity of the data obtained was supported by the high mortality figure obtained by this method for the individuals in the innermost 500-meter ring. It could then be calculated that 25.5 per cent of the total population (64,600 persons) had been killed, 27 per cent had been injured, and 47.5 per cent had escaped physically unscathed. Against the total mortality curve data obtained from special groups such as the Otake workmen could also be plotted.

November 22: Thanksgiving Day. Had a long discussion with Colonel Oughterson concerning the termination of this study, which is now clearly in sight. The shielding survey has now been completed. What remains to be done is the general casualty study. This has now been thoroughly discussed, and the detail has been designed by Lieutenant Habel, in consultation with Lieutenant Nisselson and Dr. Masuyama. The final report will be written in Washington at the Army Institute of Pathology, and George LeRoy and I will be assigned to do it, with whatever help we need. The question arises of how to return the mass of records, slides, and tissues that have now been accumulated to the U.S. I suggest that the best way would be to send them sealed to the chief surgeon's office in Tokyo through USSBS for consignment to the AIP. Then Colonel Oughterson departed for Kure to investigate the possibilities with USSBS which is based there. Upon his return he has made a tentative arrangement with the USSBS to carry the records to Tokyo for delivery to Colonel LeRoy, who will have returned by that time. The ship is the USS *Haines*, a destroyer escort vessel converted for transport, now called an APD. Lieutenant McCarthy, supply officer of the *Haines*, will take custody.

Our numbers have now been reduced, but there are still enough to make a merry feast of Ten-in-One rations with its excellent canned chicken—a not too bad substitute for turkey. The delicious Japanese tangerines add gaiety in substitution for cranberry sauce.

November 23: In the morning, arranged for packing of all our records, photographs, and slides. Then by jeep to Kure. There were hundreds of vessels in the broad harbor, and the USS *Haines* was invisible, overshadowed by the towering hulks of transports and warships. Conversation with the shore patrol reveals that the only way to locate the vessel is from a chart on the command ship. They hail the launch which plies between ship and shore. This quickly brings me to the command ship, the massive, spic-and-span cruiser *Oklahoma City*. As a lieutenant colonel I was piped aboard and, keeping what little I knew of naval etiquette in mind, saluted the flag at the stern and then the officer of the deck, who ushered me into the captain's austere presence. The USS *Haines* was quickly found on the detailed map that indicated the position of every vessel in the harbor. The captain invited me to the officers' mess for coffee and then graciously sent me to the *Haines* in his gig. The *Haines*, as a DE, was much broader than she looked from the water. Lieutenant Commander Laurent was in command, but Lieutenant McCarthy, who was to receive the consignment of records, was ashore and due to return later in the afternoon. Although there was much pressing business back in Hiroshima, I decided to stay aboard to make detailed arrangements with him. Members of the USSBS who were there told me of their fascinating experiences throughout Japan and also of the difficulties of the land-lubber's life aboard a DE, converted or not. Finally Lieutenant McCarthy arrived. We discussed the techniques of packing and trans-shipment. I indicated also that we would like to send our Sergeant Buckles back to Tokyo on the ship so that the material could be delivered in person to Colonel LeRoy. Lieutenant McCarthy said that this could be arranged with proper orders. Since the *Haines* was to sail within a few days we decided that it would be best to bring the crates, and to have Sergeant Buckles aboard tomorrow if possible. After more coffee we parted, Lieutenant McCarthy promising to have us met at the dock in the late afternoon tomorrow.

Before leaving Kure I picked up two five-gallon water cans for shipping the wet tissues.

Saturday, November 24: The day was spent in arranging all of the material systematically and in making a manifest of the records, tissues, photographs, and other materials. The tissues were wrapped in gauze, labeled with waterproof tags, and put in formalin in the water cans. Everything was finally accomplished. The boxes were nailed shut with corners painted according to specifications. On our way to the ship we stopped at Kure to see Lieutenant Colonel Hall concerning the return of Sergeant Buckles to Tokyo. This was quickly accomplished, and Buckles and the boxes were brought to the dock, where Lieutenant McCarthy graciously took all in charge, after signing for the latter.

Sunday, November 25: This was a red-letter day, since Gen. Hugh Morgan and Col. Francis Dieuaide, consultants to the surgeon general, were scheduled to arrive for a visit. Colonel Mason and I therefore went to Kure, but these gentlemen were nowhere to be found. After an idle morning we returned. We again discussed with Colonel Oughterson the closing of the establishment at Ujina. This would rest on me after the others had gone. We have considerable borrowed equipment that must be returned to the units that had given it to us on loan with the firm understanding that it would be returned at the completion of the work. Japanese equipment that had been borrowed from Tokyo Imperial University must also be sent back. After closing the laboratory at Ujina there would remain only the population study, which would proceed under Dr. Masuyama and Lieutenant Habel, and the work of collecting records and materials from other institutions. Dr. Ishii and I, who were now close friends, would travel together by jeep.

Our first stop is to be Okayama, where both the university and the Military Hospital are said to have many records. We were informed that the numerous landslides that have occurred in the mountainous country to the north after the September and October rain have made road travel between Hiroshima and Okayama all but impossible. The railroads, however, have been kept in running order, and we are advised to send the jeep by flatcar and to proceed to Okayama by train. We would then go cross-country to join the group at Kyoto. It is obvious also that considerable work will have to be done upon returning to Tokyo, especially to complete the collection of building plans of those structures in which the protection studies were done. Dr. Tsuzuki has assured us that these would be available in Tokyo, since plans for public utility and hospital buildings would have been kept in central offices there. Then took the short trip out of town to the Kaitaichi railroad station and made tentative arrangements to get men and equipment on the train.

After supper Colonel Oughterson is in a philosophical mood. I remind him of my desire to return as soon as the job in Japan is completed. He promises to make appropriate arrangements in the surgeon's office upon his imminent return to headquarters in Tokyo. We discuss also at length what we have learned of Japan and of the influence of the emperor. Scotty assures us from what he has been able to observe on his trips to Tokyo that MacArthur is held in great respect and is doing a remarkable job without the slightest sign of vindictiveness and with Japan's future recovery foremost in mind. This has been making a tremendous impression on the people, who can hardly believe it.

Monday, November 26: In the early morning, made another trip to Kaitaichi station and arranged for the departure of our personnel to Kyoto and Tokyo and for the transportation to Tokyo of the large quantities of Japanese laboratory and other equipment that had been loaned to us and have now been crated at Ujina. It was to be sent in a closed boxcar, and Lieutenant Habel was to be at the receiving end in order to release it from custody. Everything was trucked down, the loading was supervised, and the boxcar was sealed. Our two junior officers left for Kyoto. Then returned to Ujina and found that General Morgan, Colonel Turner, and Colonel Dieuaide had arrived. Lunch was prepared. It was a particular pleasure to renew acquaintance with Colonel Dieuaide, whom I had met many months previously in New Zealand, where he was making a consultant's tour. We then took the senior officers on the VIP tour of the city, through all of the selected places. General Morgan was my guest—a dignified, gray-haired figure of heroic dimensions who looked the part of senior consultant. On the way I presented to him some more details of the plan of the study and what had been accomplished. When we came to the "Korean Building," in order to gain an advantageous view of the city, I found that things had changed for the worse since my last visit. It was most revolting that the landings had been used as surface toilets. The General stepped gingerly and kept a stiff upper lip, and was rewarded by seeing the railing shadows, which were still quite clear and sharp, although the penumbra was fading in the cement at the top. He marveled at the energy of the people who were beginning to return to the sites of their homes. Rude shelters were springing up amid the rubble, walled and covered with bits of rusted corrugated metal, but still the beginnings of a rebirth. To our disappointment the shadows on the bridge were now only faintly visible, but they impressed the general. Our visitors then returned to Kure with Colonel Turner. It was now getting dark and beginning to drizzle slightly. Then home to a delightful steaming bath.

One important item that I had promised to Dr. Shigeto remained to be completed: the protocol of an autopsy done on a girl, Fusako Tsuta, who had been a patient at the Red Cross Hospital. The slides were now completed. The death, as we expected, was not clearly related to the atomic-bomb injury, but rather to typhoid fever. The microscopic descriptions were completed and typed out by Sergeant Huffaker. Then we cooked some bacon and eggs and brought Colonels Oughterson and Mason to the railroad station to see them off on the night train. Fond goodnights and Godspeed were said. Colonel Mason was bound for Kyoto and Scotty for Tokyo.

CHAPTER 5

Mopping Up

November 27: The final closing of the shop was the order of the day. The first item of business was to return the refrigerator to the ambulance company. This was done with the willing help of our remaining enlisted men, who were eager to return closer to civilization. The refrigerator had been a trustworthy servant throughout our stay. Then to Kure, where Sergeant Huffaker, who had performed splendidly, was left at his new assignment at the 361st Station Hospital. Colonel Mason's curette and my autopsy kit were also left there, and the radio was returned to the tender mercies of the I & E officers. Then hurried back to Ujina for Ishii and our luggage. Ishii and I made the train scheduled for 2:58 P.M. The jeep was put on a flatcar. The trip from Kure was through a country of sharply pyramidal terraced hills, looking like the lovely islands in the inland sea.

We arrived at 7:20 P.M. The jeep was ready for use. When I opened the front compartment I found that the copy of Wintrobe's *Hematology* that I had put there was missing. I then looked in the metal compartment in the back seat, also unlocked, but all of the numerous cans of chicken from the Ten-in-One rations that we had stored there were still intact. This was ironic, since the chicken would have made a much more digestible diet for hungry people than the Wintrobe. We did not have an easy time finding lodgings for Dr. Ishii. We stopped at a Japanese hotel, but there was no room. We became thoroughly confused trying to find the Okayama Japanese Military Hospital from directions that Ishii had obtained but finally obtained a place of lodging there for him. Then went in search of the Twenty-first Regimental Combat Team stationed in Okayama and found it after considerable difficulty. I was given a place in No. 18, a "guest room," bare and cold except for a small charcoal fire in a brazier. Then some writing of these notes and wearily to bed.

November 28: In the morning met General Miura, a friend and former co-worker of Professor Tsuzuki. Through Ishii, he extended his cooperation and was all politeness. A number of patients from Hiroshima were in this hospital. We photographed several and then went to inspect the laboratory. Some gross material was there which after considerable discussion was shared, as had been agreed. Again we emphasized that they were free to prepare their own reports on their own observations. At Okayama University we were received by Dr. Tanabe, a pathologist. He seemed a charming person who offered every help for our work, including a large room with his personal electric heater. This was gratefully received, since the weather was raw. Went to work with Dr. Ishii on the translation of the autopsy protocols that were available both from the Military Hospital and from the University files. Two of the more important are still missing. Again it was interesting to observe that when our attitude was made known and the hand of friendship extended it was gladly seized. Again "home" after much Japanese tea and conversation. The officers of the Combat Team were a gruff but friendly lot, and not very communicative. They seemed to accept quite philosophically their assignment on that frigid plateau in the two-thirds-destroyed city. Their disposition to share their whisky was helpful.

November 29: Dr. Ishii and I worked through the day translating the autopsy material records. Late in the afternoon we were introduced to Professor Tsuda, the head of the Department of Surgery at the University of Okayama. He has the most ornate office that I have seen in Japan to date. He and his staff had taken care of some of the evacuees from Hiroshima. Later in the afternoon Dr. Tamagawa, who had previously visited at Hiroshima, fulfilled his agreement to share with us material from a number of autopsies he had performed both at Hiroshima and at Okayama. Dr. Tsuda gave us permission to take his clinical records to Kyoto, where it would be more convenient to transcribe them and where there would be more help. We were now more free to concentrate on the Military Hospital records.

November 30: Translations continued. We found certain discrepancies in previously abstracted charts from the Okayama Military Hospital, and consequently reviewed the original records with special care. Slides already prepared were given to us from a number of cases by Professor Tanabe. A few more not currently available are to be cut and sent to us. We were now ready to continue our journey. Again packed up our belongings and new acquisitions for an early start on the following morning.

Saturday, December 1: Started at exactly 6:30 on the long road to Kyoto. Ishii was ready and waiting when I called for him. It was a sparkling clear day after a very threatening afternoon on the day before. The weather was freezing cold and it was difficult to keep warm while driving in the open jeep even in the brilliant sunshine. The trip was through rough high country, with the roads still interrupted by washouts created by the fall rains; the roads were sometimes negotiable by jeep, but on occasion required detours. Many stops are made for discussions of the best way across the mountains from village to village by Dr. Ishii. The people were curious but very friendly, since there has been almost no penetration by American occupation forces into this territory. At about 9:30 we stopped for breakfast in the sunlight and to thaw out a little bit in the courtyard of a farmhouse. We were most graciously received by a delightful peasant family who prepared some hot tea for us. They also seemed very appreciative of our own food that we induced them to share with us. We departed good friends, leaving some packages of chocolate and cigarettes. As the day warmed, the trip through the mountainous Hyōgo prefecture became even more delightful. There were sharp ridges and peaks covered by the deep green of pine forests, rising above terraced paddies full of dark water that reflected mountains and brilliant sky. Our progress toward Himeji was slow because of the detours. We entered this beautiful city at about noon. Here there was a storybook castle reminiscent of the one at Hiroshima, as seen in pre-war photographs. The building, gleaming white, rises to a tower of many levels, with sweeping graceful gray tile-covered roofs and an ornate top story. We took time to explore the building, which within actually is a simple wooden structure with rough walls. Ishii told me that truly ancient castles are rare in Japan since fires, on the average, burn the Japanese cities at eight-year intervals. The castle is set in a lovely park of grass and trees that adds to its beauty. We left Himeji reluctantly and proceeded along a splendid road to Kobe, which we reached one-and-a-half hours later. This is a large commercial center, much of it devastated by bombing and fire. Kyoto was not far, and we made off along a crowded highway to reach our destination at about 4:00 P.M. The surgeon's office was at Sixth Army headquarters, which occupied a tremendous black building, the Daikan. In the surgeon's office was Col. M. Dawson Tyson, whose name was quite familiar although I had never met him. He had been on the house staff in pathology at Yale before continuing in surgery. In civilian life he had been one of the senior surgeons at the Hitchcock Hospital in Hanover, New Hampshire, where there was a large nucleus of Yale-educated medical men. I was assigned a room at the Biwako, but before proceeding there it was necessary first to find quarters for Dr. Ishii. Suitable lodgings were found at a rambling Japanese hotel labeled "Off Limits." An additional difficulty was that Major Kramer and Captain Rosenbaum and Loge were quartered beyond the center of the city in a tall, white, commercial-looking building reminiscent of the Dai Ichi. At long last, found Jack Rosenbaum and the others. They reported that they had made excellent progress in collecting and transcribing the clinical data and that there were only a few more days of work left to do. We went to the Miyako, the most splendid hotel in the city, used for senior officers' quarters. We all enjoyed the reunion over cocktails and a delightful supper of roast beef. The usefulness of having our own transportation now became obvious, since I discovered that the Biwako was far out of town, on Lake Biwa. It was dark, and the map was difficult to follow after leaving the main road. There were a few small signs in English which had be read by flashlight, but at long last the hotel was found on what seemed to be a small island connected with a bridge to the mainland. This was obviously a resort, and I was given an immense double room with private bath. There crisp, clean sheets and the soft mattress soon received a tired body. Entertainment was in progress and the music of the *samisen* was a lullaby only briefly heard. It all seemed like a dream after Hiroshima.

Sunday, December 2: Woke rather late but refreshed. Happily, breakfast was still being most graciously served by persons who behaved like courtiers. The Biwako was indeed lovely throughout, with huge common rooms and delightful lawns and gardens. From my second-floor window the lofty hills on the far side of the lake were reflected in the blue water. Since I knew we would have much to do in Kyoto and since I had not met the surgeon in command I returned to headquarters. To my surprise, even the senior officers were there. I was introduced to General Hagins. The general was a bit suspicious of our mission, since the intact and lovely city of Kyoto had become a mecca for those of the military desiring a real taste of Japanese life in its pre-war state. I informed him that all of this had happened while our backs were turned on the rest of the country during our labors and that our major aim was to obtain materials and records from various Japanese institutions. I then became the recipient of a one-and-one-half-hour lecture on the world in general, and especially on how wicked the Negroes were. I was anxious to leave his office to visit the Kyoto University, where Ishii had told me a pathology meeting was to be in progress. Many of the senior pathologists of Japan were there. I had the pleasure of meeting at once Dr. Riojun Kinoshita, who was presiding. He spoke English beautifully. They repaired to Chinese restaurants in the vicinity, which were in operation but, unfortunately, off-limits to military personnel, and I had to content myself with the remnants of a K ration. The grounds of the university were delightful in the bright sunshine, and the lunch was enjoyed in solitude. Then returned to the meeting, where some beautiful pathology was shown. Among the finest demonstrations, the lectures being incomprehensible to me, was that of Hamazaki, who spoke on cytological details in diseased tissue. It was a pleasure also to meet the world-famous hematologist of the university, Dr. Amano, who seemed reserved and depressed. I was told that he had been with the group that had been lost in the landslide during the typhoon of mid-September.

Dr. Kinoshita said he had several autopsy cases from Hiroshima available and invited me to visit his institute at Osaka. I had to leave before Professor Tanabe, who was speaking, was finished, but ultimately the slides that he had promised reached me through the kind offices of Dr. Ishii. Late in the afternoon, had supper at the Miyako with Colonel Mason. While there bought another beautiful *satsuma* powder box and some wooden bamboo cigarette cases. Most important of all was a lovely string of pearls, designed for C. G.

Colonel Mason had already investigated all of the local stores and provided me with details, as well as with a map. Then home to the Biwako through the dark but still lovely countryside.

December 3: Early in the morning, went to meet the physicians at the Prefectural Hospital. We were well received, and they gave us all of the gross material from the few cases that were available. At this time also saw for the first time films that had been made by the staff by exposing roentgen films to the bones of the bomb victims. These seem to be artifacts, since the outline of the bone was sharp, and translucent in contrast with the black of the rest of the film. At headquarters in the later morning was interrogated at length by Lieutenant Colonel Bogue of G2, who delved thoroughly into my past history, recent and old, apparently considering our whole mission suspect. I produced a copy of our orders of October 12 and informed him that all cooperation would be expected, or I would find it necessary to communicate directly with headquarters in Tokyo. This produced a marvelous effect, since the requirement for assistance from the Sixth Army was quite clearly indicated.

Called on Professor Amano in his crowded laboratory at the Kyoto University. We had a somewhat halting discussion, since his English was far from fluent. Dr. Ishii was most helpful throughout. After some hesitation Professor Amano informed me that the hematology slides of the three earliest cases which had been autopsied at Ninoshima would be made available. I then asked him to collect this material for the following morning by 9 A.M. Dr. Funaoka, the professor of anatomy, was also consulted, and stated that some of the autopsy material was still at Kanazawa University, on the western side of the country, but that he would telephone to expedite the transmittal of the material. The late Professor Sugiyama had taught at Kanazawa in the past.

December 4: Promptly in the morning, went with Dr. Ishii and received the slides from Dr. Amano. He appeared to be a very sad man indeed, and recounted how he had lost his wife and child. When we went to see Dr. Funaoka he regretfully said that he had not had a reply from Kanazawa but that the material would be forthcoming, perhaps by 3:00 P.M. In the meantime we had been invited by Dr.

Amano to visit a Mrs. Miura, who was German and who wished to meet an American.

At her home we were served a delightful tea, with German kuchen. The conversation also was bilingual, in German with me and in Japanese with Drs. Amano and Ishii. A very pleasant interlude.

When we returned to Dr. Funaoka's office at the university were glad to find that the slides had indeed arrived from Kanazawa. However, the gross material had been taken away by Lieutenant Colonel French, who was conducting a survey of Japanese laboratories for SCAP. This put an additional complication into the problem, but we had some confidence that this aspect could be rectified ultimately. Gradually various local intricacies came to light: Dr. Amano also proved to have some slides of the Ono cases. Dr. Fukutani, a member of the same department, had additional slides on the same cases, but from different organs! Also, Dr. Fukutani had all of the Ushida slides. This remarkable fact resulted from misunderstandings that followed the early happy leadership of Sugiyama, a fine hematologist and pathologist who had been a student of Professor Kiyono, after whom the institute at Kyoto was named. A further complication was that a member of the Kyoto group had been asked to leave the autopsy room at Nagasaki because, without permission, he had apparently begun to tamper with some of the material that had been acquired by Comdr. Shields Warren. The matter was finally resolved by asking Dr. Ishii to call Professor Mori, the chief of the Institute of Pathology, on the telephone in order to request his help in obtaining representative slides. This was finally accomplished and the mystery of the errant slides was finally solved. A number of the slides required remounting because they had become stuck together. We said that we would return on the sixth for these.

December 5: I left Dr. Ishii in Kyoto to complete the haggling about the slides in his own quiet and efficient manner and went with Dr. Ishikawa to keep my appointment with Professor Kinoshita in Osaka. On the way we stopped at the Takatsuke Medical School to pick up two important cases for the Nagasaki group. There we met Dr. Eguchi, who was very gracious and gave me, without stint, all of his important material and an excellent set of clinical and pathological records and slides. While there Dr. Ishikawa volunteered the information he had just acquired from Dr. Eguchi, that Dr. Kuno of the Japanese Naval Hospital at Iwakuni, who still had in his possession some of the best of the early material, was living nearby. We went on a most interesting hunt through the residential districts and finally found Dr. Kuno's wife and charming daughter and father in a clean and lovely Japanese home. There, after introductions and tea, a long letter was left by Dr. Ishikawa in the hope that it would be answered by Dr. Kuno.

We proceeded to Osaka and, after dinner in a small Japanese restaurant fortunately not labeled off-limits, went on to see Dr. Kinoshita at his department. He was most cordial and after delivering a tirade against the mix-up caused by Colonel French's intervention, through no fault of his own, finally produced the specimens that were needed. These included both gross and microscopic material. He discussed some of his own investigative work on nutrition. One set of studies was made on prisoners who had a reasonably constant diet of rice and beans and certain vegetables to a total of 2,200 calories daily, with 110 grams of protein. They, however, developed edema and, in some instances, a "cachectic" type of malnutrition. When five grams of gelatin were given daily good health was restored, or the condition could be prevented if prisoners were fed gelatin initially. He had continued his researches. Among other pieces of research were: (1) Work on the histogenesis of chicken sarcomas. He believed that they arise from adventitial cells. (2) In the butter-yellow work that had gained him worldwide fame, catalase may be used as an index of whether or not the liver is going to become cancerous: it decreases sharply long before the tumor is grossly detectable. Dr. Kinoshita had been in the United States many times, had a Caucasian wife, and was fully familiar with the Western world.

Then, after a very long and wearing but remarkably interesting day, back along the busy road to Kyoto through the gathering dark.

December 6: On this, which was to be our last day in Kyoto, found that our Japanese colleagues had already purchased tickets and that there was no problem in getting them "home" in the morning. Went again to the university, received the bone-marrow slides from Dr. Amano, and also called on Dr. Funaoka, who was not there. I was, however, advised that his material would be in readiness later in the afternoon. Another long talk was had with Dr. Amano concerning hematology in general. He seemed most pleased at the gift of soap and butter and eggs that I had brought for Mrs. Miura.

[Professor Amano had been an author, with Professors Kiyono and Sugiyama, of an outstanding book, published in 1938, *Die Lehre der Vitalfärbung*. Since the war he has written a large hematology text of his own.]

Early in the afternoon I finally went to the finance office and discovered that I was owed what seemed to me the enormous sum of 11,253 yen, which included approximately $220 worth of undeserved per diem. This was a somewhat illogical, but nevertheless useful, consequence of orders to live in a place where it was almost impossible to spend money and where we were almost completely isolated and confined to standard field rations. With this tremendous amount of money in hand, I was ready to buy a few little things, and this was accomplished in a trip about the city with Dr. Loge—a silver cigarette box, a lovely *satsuma* bowl hand-decorated and now scarce, and a red lacquer tray and bowls. Then rushed back to the Biwako, signed out, and quickly packed all belongings; then to the train. There was a long but not too unpleasant wait in the station. The berths in the Japanese trains were comfortable, but four men were in a single room, and only one at a time could dress.

December 7: On this anniversary arrived again in Tokyo about one-and-a-half hours late, found the surgeon's office, and received at once a courteous offer of transportation. In the meantime took a "taxi jeep" to obtain our own jeep at the Shiodome yards, which I thought might have arrived by this time. It was there but would not start, and had to be dragged off the flatcar. Inspection revealed that the rotor had been taken out and that some of the wires had been stripped. There was nothing to do but walk back to the surgeon's office and obtain transportation after signing in. A blessed quantity of mail was waiting. I was pleased again to be assigned to my old home, the Dai Ichi. Obtained room 858, which was sans bath, but a room with bath was promised soon. In the middle of the afternoon met Lieutenant Colonel Barnacle, who was taking the chief surgeon's place pro tem. He was in every way kind and pleasant. Colonel Oughterson was there and seemed satisfied with the ultimate outcome of the work. He also said that we would be ordered back just as soon as he had returned to the United States.

December 8: Our records had been delivered to an office in the surgeon's division that was to be assigned to me for the remainder of my time. Went to the university and found Dr. Hatano, who wanted to take me to the Tokyo First Military Hospital. At the university, also met Dr. Tsuzuki, who, to my surprise, was performing a hysterectomy, and Dr. Mitani. Dr. Mitani offered me his sword and said this was a family heirloom, an "old sword" made at least 400 years ago of drawn Damascus steel. The scabbard and handle, he said, were modern and without particular worth. I said that I should be glad to keep the weapon for him in token of our friendship but that I would wish to return it when the political circumstances again permitted. He said that he considered it a symbol of militarism and that he no longer wanted it in his family and would turn it over to me in a few days.

At the hospital it was a pleasure to meet again General Hirai and Major Misono, and, for the first time, Major Ohashi, a pathologist who had done many of the autopsies at Ujina during September. All promised to have prepared the autopsy tissues that had been cut in Tokyo, which were related to the protocols that we had been translating in Hiroshima with Dr. Ishii. An appointment was made for Monday morning to meet these gentlemen again, when everything was to be in readiness. General Hirai promised to have material from the patients autopsied by Major Yamashina on Ninoshima Island in the first few days after the bombing. I had already received some of this material from Dr. Amano, including bone marrows and certain tissues obtained by the late Dr. Sugiyama. Dr. Hatano also said that Dr. Kusano of the Tokyo Infectious Disease Institute had done some autopsies at Saijyo on Hiroshima patients and that he would gladly give us material. We then went by jeep in search of the institute but had failed by closing time and returned, somewhat disgustedly, home.

December 9: Drs. Oughterson and LeRoy had received orders to return and were to leave tomorrow. George LeRoy's father was ill. After packing a number of items to be brought back personally by

Dr. Oughterson, spent the afternoon at the zoo with Major Kramer, and then wandered through the beautiful park on the crisp afternoon. Then a quiet evening at home, broken only by a gay celebration in honor of those departing. At least some of us were on the homecoming path.

December 10, 1945–January 25, 1946: It would be best to summarize rather than to give a daily account of what seemed to be an endless time in Tokyo before orders came to return. One name and one number on the endless roster of those with the same desire has a special importance only to oneself. Had I then more of the philosophy of the country where I was now an enforced guest, and were there not a special wedding to attend more than 7,000 miles away, I would have taken more joy in the privilege that was mine. During this time there was opportunity for becoming better acquainted in their own setting with the brilliant men of Japan who had worked so diligently with us at Hiroshima—a fact that I did appreciate then, and value even more highly now. Many have indeed fulfilled the promise implied in Professor Tsuzuki's choice of them for this work twenty years ago, when they were very young men, and they now occupy positions of leadership in Japanese medicine.

As it was, there were still two weeks of labor to gather up the loose ends. On Monday, December 10, at another visit to the Tokyo First Military Hospital, the autopsy material was indeed ready. It included the three earliest cases autopsied by Major Yamashina. At this time also, Major Motohashi showed me some superb photographs of patients with petechiae, ulcerative lesions of the mucous membranes, and epilation from the earlier Ujina series. He said that they had all the prints required and graciously presented the glass negatives. I did finally have the pleasure of meeting Dr. Kusano at the Institute for Infectious Diseases, and he likewise supplied the Saijyo material. Our records, histological slides, and gross tissues were now largely in order, except that we had very little material on the eyes.

Although interesting effects on the eyes had been described by the well-known ophthalmologist Dr. Takehisa Oguchi (after whom a hereditary type of nyctalopia has been named), working at the Kaijin Kai Hospital in Kure, and although extensive notes had been taken by Dr. Mason, we had almost no tissue. On inquiry of our good

Dr. Jasushi Mitani
Department of Obs. & Gyn.
Osaka National University
Osaka, Japan

Dear Dr. Mitani:

You may recall that you entrusted your family sword to my possession during the days of our co-operation in Hiroshima. I have always considered this a trusteeship of an heirloom, to the time when it might be possible to return it.

It may, of course, be that you no longer have an interest in such a military symbol. In that instance, I intend to keep it as a memento of a busy and happy time that we had working and studying together.

I am very much interested in how you are getting on in our present activities.

With every good wish.

Yours sincerely,

Averill A. Liebow, M.D.
John Slade Ely Professor of Pathology

AAL:st

The author's letter offering to return Professor Mitani's family sword.

Professor Mitani's answer to Dr. Liebow's letter.

44 Motoomachi
Nagasaki, Japan

July 15, 1957

Dear Dr. Liebow:

I have just read with pleasure your letter which was forwarded from Osaka University to me. I beg your pardon for my long silence. I have always recollected your kindness and courtesy during the days of our cooperation in Hiroshima.

I know that you are now working especially on lung-pathology.

Concerning the sword which I presented you before, I hope you keep it as an expression of my appreciation.

I was appointed as a professor of Nagasaki University in 1947 and have worked to reestablish our department.

After coming to Nagasaki Mrs. Mitani had suffered from pulmonary tuberculosis for a few years, but she has recovered from it completely and is now enjoying complete health except decrease of vital capacity caused by thoracoplastic operation. Our only son Hiroshi is now attending to the school of technology of Tokyo University and is expected to be graduated from it the next March.

I myself have been always healthy, grew fat and my hair has become thinner. I am now majoring in uterine cancer and chorionepithelioma malignum and have published several works on them. Most of them were published in Japanese and I don't think it adequate to present you those copies. But I should like to present you some copies of our works published in English under separate cover, and hope they will be of some use to you.

I suppose you have several children by now, and I hope your family are well and happy. I hope to have the opportunity to see you again in the near future.

Yours sincerely,

Y. Mitani

Yasushi Mitani, M.D.
Professor of Obstetrics & Gynecology,
Nagasaki University

friend Professor Miyake, with whom I had briefly discussed the subject before, I found that Professor Shoji of the Eye Institute and he were planning a collaborative study of the eyes, but that the sections had not as yet been prepared. Professor Miyake said that he was planning to share this material when it had been embedded in celloidin and cut, and these blocks did indeed reach us some six months later.

I was also informed that a documentary film had been prepared at Hiroshima by the Nippon Eigasha late in August 1945, but that this had not been completely developed. After much discussion with Messrs. Kobayama and Aihara of that company, the film was developed, and on December 19 it was viewed in the surgeon's office. As expected, it was a remarkable record. Its possible use for propaganda purposes was also not difficult to visualize. The film had been made on nitrate rather than safety stock, but a copy was retained and sent to the United States for use by the American component of the Joint Commission.

Of greatest help in obtaining the all-important building plans were Drs. Murai and Murachi. Those of the broadcasting station were the first to come to hand, on December 10. Within another week blueprints of the Communication Department buildings were located. This represented the bulk of the material needed. Those of the Central Telephone Office were found later, and those of the Bankers' Club were located after considerable detective work on the part of Drs. Murai and Murachi at the architect's office in Osaka, and were subsequently delivered. In the meantime, many informative discussions were held with these two remarkable men, who had been calculating shielding factors in a preliminary way. They were also most kind in showing me much of Tokyo that I would have missed otherwise.

On December 14 all of the Americans of the Joint Commission who remained were entertained at a splendid dinner at the Military Hospital, with all of our Japanese colleagues in the military and many of the younger civilians in attendance. There was plenty of *Suntory*, a fine whiskey with the taste of Scotch. The best of the traditional Japanese dishes were served, complete with entrees of raw fish and squid, and endless quantities of warm *sake* to wash the many courses down. The spirit was a token of comradeship based on personal understanding that developed under stress and on recognition of merit and that crossed barriers of race and politics. More than this, it was a tribute to the wisdom of Ashley W. Oughterson that the younger of us may not have possessed.

As to our personal affairs, we learned for ourselves what has long been known—that there is nothing more irksome than a delay in getting home after a long war. Mustering out on "points," of which we had a great sufficiency, could have been arranged at once, yet this would preclude fulfilling our responsibility for writing the report. The matter was especially complicated in my case since certain notes were still in shorthand. When Colonel Schwichtenberg returned on December 12 he reiterated what Scotty had said, that we would have to await orders from Washington. We were relieved to discover that someone had thought to assign us to the Eighth Army, since our original orders had called for our return to our original stations, which in our case would have been the Marianas—perish the thought. We therefore presented ourselves to ASCOM in Yokohama and were delighted to find Brig. Gen. Earl Maxwell in charge. General Maxwell had been the chief surgeon of the army in the South Pacific, where I had come to know him well. He and Colonel Snyder were sympathetic and said that they would take good care of us while we were in Japan. Lieut. Phil Loge, soon to be captain, was assigned to the Forty-second General Hospital in Tokyo, where he was very happy and where we all spent many pleasant evenings later. Major Kramer was made chief of the Medical Service at the 334th Station Hospital in Yokohama. Rosenbaum and myself were to be left to our own devices in the chief surgeon's office in Tokyo for the moment. Later Rosenbaum was assigned, "condemned," as he put it, to the 334th. General Maxwell invited Jack and me to dinner on the following evening in his quarters at the New Grand in Yokohama, an establishment of faded but substantial splendor that had been MacArthur's first home on his return to Japan. The general, always good company, was at his best and was reinforced by Colonel DeLorimier, chief of the Army School of Roentgenology. We particularly enjoyed reminiscing about personalities in the Yale Hospital Unit as it had been in the South Pacific, and particularly about Cols. Paul Harper and Scotty Oughterson. The evening did much to bolster our spirits, but it was still only December 12, and we were destined for a long wait.

Contacts with Dr. Ishii were only occasional, as he was busy with his own affairs. It was on Saturday, December 15, when he presented me with two things—a treasure of a blue and red obi for my bride, and the letter in which he told for the first time of his plight. Successful efforts were made to obtain a position for him, and thereafter, having survived a siege of typhoid, possibly acquired during the memorable autopsy on the young patient from the Red Cross Hospital in Hiroshima, things began to go better. He was appointed to the professorship of pathology at Shinshu University in Matsumoto.

We made the best of Tokyo, enjoying the sights and sounds of this great capital. Among the most pleasant were made by the violinist Mari Iwamoto, by the Nippon Symphony, now revived, and by a choir, mixed Japanese and American, singing the Messiah together. In the interval of three months since our coming, the city was showing definite signs of recovery. Much of the rubble had been cleared. Scaffolding, often a spiderwork cunningly fashioned of bamboo, was rising, and stone and concrete were filling old wounds. Shops were bright with wares. Christmas came and the Dai Ichi building across the moat from the Imperial palace was swathed in green and illuminated, somewhat garishly, like a card. On the sparkling afternoon of January 1 a vast crowd, the ladies now for the first time in public dressed in colorful kimonos, stood in a respectful, almost worshipful, silence as General MacArthur arrived at his headquarters. The New Year's greeting on the building seemed to be intended for civilians as well as for the occupation forces.

Without sign or sound from Washington and the first weeks of the New Year gone, I was tempted to accept an opening for a return passage as commanding officer of a hospital ship, a purely administrative post, but one that would have brought me home by way of Okinawa and taken at least thirty days. It is good to report that a more temperate judgment prevailed, for on the twentieth, in response to the urgings of Colonel Schwichtenberg at this end and possibly from the patient Oughterson at the other, the blessed orders came. Although most of the Commission's impedimenta had gone back, I had retained enough records to keep myself occupied in preparing some drafts of portions of the final report. These, plus the slides and records and blueprints and the tissues more recently acquired, made a sizable package of some 250 pounds, which was

Members of the Joint Commission, December 1945. From left to right: Lieut. J. Philip Loge, the late Maj. Milton L. Kramer, and the late Capt. Jack D. Rosenbaum.

sealed in a trunk labeled "Secret" and returned with me as courier, at a high priority. The difficulties of the return were minor indeed, compared to its joys. There were, inevitably, engine repairs on our elderly C-54 at Kwajalein; a very unmilitary customs officer at Honolulu asking suspiciously whether there were any seeds or feathers in the sealed and inviolable trunk, and sniffing, to my embarrassment, at the soiled and atom-burned clothing in my personal luggage. But then fresh Hawaiian pineapple and scenery for a day; two days in San Francisco; and at last a landing in four inches of snow at the Washington National Airport at 1:00 A.M. on a Saturday morning. For a time we considered ourselves lucky, for the pilot was on the point of returning across the Alleghenies, but he decided to chance it, and won. Although the airport was cozy enough, Washington snowstorms in 1946, even more than now, had the unhappy effect of isolating us. I put my sealed trunk in charge of the security officer and decided to doze until the thaws came. Only the arrival of Gen. Joe Collins on a later flight saved us. He had been commander of the Twenty-fifth Division, and we had met him many times as a frequent visitor to the Thirty-ninth General Hospital. The general, with his customary grace, delivered some of us to our hotel, the Sheraton Park, in his staff car and ordered the driver to come back until all were rescued. The warm bed was welcome, but even more the joy of being back at last.

The Dai Ichi Building, headquarters of SCAP, decorated for New Year's Day, January 1, 1946.

A part of the immense crowd awaiting the arrival of General MacArthur on New Year's Day, 1946. The women are wearing gay kimonos for the first time in public since the bombing.

CHAPTER 6

Q. E. F.

Early on the morning of January 28, when I reported for duty, as
ordered, to Col. James Earl Ash, commanding officer of the Army
Institute of Pathology, I saluted as smartly as I could. This courtly
gentleman was astonished but regained his composure sufficiently to
return the courtesy. Forgiveness was not long in coming, and he said
that he had been expecting me and that Colonel LeRoy and I had been
assigned a special room for our work. This was a large chamber
separated from the remainder of the second floor of the wonderful
old Army Institute of Pathology by a ten-foot wall. Thus immured,
our records could stay in the required security. The Institute, located
at Seventh Street and Independence Avenue, with its back to the
mall, was a structure dating back to a time not long after the Civil
War, with the large windows and pleasant inconveniences charac-
teristic of that era. Enclosed in its dingy but glowing dark-red brick
and musty woodwork were one of the greatest medical libraries in
the world and the treasures, old and new, of Army medicine. Here
the relics of Lincoln's assassination were reverently preserved, together with medical mementoes and records of all the wars. But more
than this, it was a treasure house of the science of pathology—an
immense storehouse of tissues and of the thoughts of the men who
had examined them. As a part of both the history of warfare and the
substance of science there was no more fitting place to which the
collection that had been gathered in Japan should be brought. Nor
was there anywhere a place better prepared to facilitate the preparation of a report. While the Institute was military in its origin and

affiliation, it had been filling an honored function as a consultation center for pathologists throughout the world. Most important was that it was permeated by the fatherly spirit of "Didi" Ash, a scholar in his own right, and it had about it an Emersonian atmosphere of "contented industry."

When I arrived, Colonel LeRoy was off to Rochester on temporary duty. It was a relief to find that everything had come safely across the Pacific. I was soon made acquainted with the procedures of the Institute. A single accession number (158930) was assigned to the entire collection, under which it remains to this day. While awaiting orders for leave, I began to unpack with the willing help of Capt. Edward B. Smith. The five-gallon water cans had served well, and the tissues were identified, blocked, and cut. Records were put in order, and everything was gotten in readiness. Discussions were held with Colonels Oughterson and Ash regarding a secretariat, which obviously would be necessary.

In the meantime I called C. G. and was pleased to discover her willingness to come to New York. Our "engagement" lasted only ten days, and we returned happily, after being married in Rochester, to Washington late in February to share the first six months of our marriage with the atomic bomb.

The first task was to decide upon the basic structure of the report, and this was done in consultation with Colonel Oughterson. Although he left the military service soon after our return, he maintained contact with us by frequent visits to Washington. It was obvious that the work would have to represent the confluence of four main streams of activity: 1) Statistical analysis of the data; 2) illustrative work; 3) the shielding study; 4) preparation of the body of the report.

Colonel Oughterson arranged for the statistical work to be done at the office of the air surgeon through the cooperation of Col. Robert E. Lyons, chief of the Biometrics Division. The Joint Commission was most fortunate to obtain the services of Maj. E. Cuyler Hammond,[*] and he was assisted by Dr. B. Aubrey Schneider, and Capt.

---

[*] Dr. Hammond's outstanding talents were later recognized by his appointment as chief statistician of the American Cancer Society, a post which he continues to hold. For a time he was also professor of statistics at Yale. Dr. Schneider died suddenly at an early age. Dr. Barnett returned to teaching at Cornell and now is chairman of the Pediatric Department at the Albert Einstein Medical School.

Henry L. Barnett. The first task was to set up a code and key, at which Dr. Hammond was a past master. It required extensive consultation on the use of terms and on the clarification of certain ambiguities, insofar as this was possible. This he obtained from Captain Barnett and from the others of us by an exchange of ideas and frequent exchange of visits across the Potomac. It was an education in itself to work with a man of Major Hammond's background, intelligence, and integrity. The results of this statistical analysis in themselves occupy one stout volume of the Joint Commission Report, which is composed chiefly of tabulated data. Many of the conclusions were also incorporated into the body of the report.

Captain Brownell was put in charge of systematizing the 1,500 photographs that had been obtained by the Joint Commission. The bulk of the material consisted of photographs made by himself and his team. In addition, many photographs had been given to the Joint Commission by several Japanese news agencies, notably Bunka-sha and Domei, and by Professor Nishina, who had been in the city within a few day of the bombing; there was also the priceless group of glass negatives presented by Major Motohashi of the Tokyo First Military Hospital. In addition, the personal 35-mm. Kodachromes that had been made by Colonel Oughterson and myself proved to be a valuable resource, since many of the larger color films in Captain Brownell's stock had been damaged, probably by heat. The small Kodachromes were enlarged and now comprise an important component of the official record. Captain Brownell personally supervised the process at the laboratories of his company, Eastman Kodak, in Rochester. He was also responsible for the reproduction and enlargement from the negatives, and the preparation of albums with appropriate identifications from which the illustrations for the final report were selected. Photomicrographs were prepared with Mr. Roy M. Reeve, a gentleman of the old school, who was also a master of the modern technology for which the Army Institute of Pathology was famous. Diagrams and charts and other art work from our crude sketches were skillfully prepared by Mr. Harry Nussbaum.

Colonel Oughterson also had arranged with the U.S. Strategic Bombing Survey to calculate the shielding factors from the various building plans that had been obtained by this group and by ourselves. We were in possession of the survival data for persons in specific positions in these buildings. These had been obtained largely through the painstaking efforts of Drs. Murachi and Murai. The arduous work of making the projections from the building plans was carried out by Lieut. Col. Herbert S. Swanson of the Corps of Engineers, assisted by a number of skilled draftsmen, in the office of Prof. Harry L. Bowman, chief of the Physical Damage Section of the USSBS, who was on loan from the University of Pittsburgh. These men were housed in temporary buildings (still standing twenty years later) next to the Washington airport. Frequent visits were made to ensure the necessary communication.

As a yokemate George LeRoy was tireless, learned, stimulating, and witty. We thoroughly enjoyed being at hard labor for six months, particularly as a semblance of order began to appear out of the great nebula of data that had been accumulated. We can say only good things about our secretaries, Mildred Broscious, Margaret Dismukes, John O'Donnell, Agnes Petsing, and Margaret Robb. They were not only efficient but uncomplaining, and had a remarkably high tolerance for persiflage. We decided that insofar as possible we would attempt to compare the effects in the two cities, writing independently but in parallel. This was possible in most of the eleven sections into which this work naturally divided itself.

Section 2 on Physics was written with the collaboration of R. E. Marshak, Ph.D., a physicist. It seemed best to combine data from the two cities on hematology and also on the bone marrow, and this section was written by LeRoy, while I took responsibility similarly for the volume on pathology. The statistical section was compiled and written by the team at the air surgeon's office, led by Cuyler Hammond.

Having established the major categories, much of the early work consisted of sorting out and systematizing. For example, the autopsy material from Hiroshima consisted of the records and slides of three of the early patients from Ninoshima, and of twelve from Ujina autopsied by Major Yamashina; eight in a later group autopsied by Major Ohashi; twenty-six by the group from Tokyo Imperial University at Ujina; two at Tokyo Imperial University itself, upon evacuees from Ujina; two performed at Ujina during the time of the Joint Commission; thirteen from Ushida; ten from Ono (Kyoto Imperial University); six from the Kyoto Prefectural University; six from Iwakuni, including several very early cases; eight from Okayama Military Hospital; one from the Okayama Medical School; twenty-one from Saijyo; nineteen from the Post Office Hospital, performed by Professor Tamagawa; one from Yodobashi Hospital in Tokyo; three from Osaka. This represented a total of 141 cases, of which two had to be discarded. Most of the protocols had already been translated and redictated into the standard form used by the Army Medical Department. Others were still in shorthand and required dictation. This was the first order of business. Later, as the slides were cut, they required study and description. The cases had to be grouped according to distance from the hypocenter and time of death, and the individual findings from the groups had to be catalogued and illustrated. Similar problems arose for most of the other sections. In many instances the completion of portions of the work by others—for example, the statistical analyses—had to be awaited and the results then incorporated into the general text.

As we wrote, ideas were exchanged, debated, and finally used or not, until a pattern emerged. This was employed to present the data from both cities whenever applicable. Drs. Oughterson and Shields Warren were frequently asked for guidance, and we were the beneficiaries of consultations wanted and unwanted from a large number of interested persons. We were also the recipients of some lessons in the cold business of war. One afternoon an officer in the Intelligence Section called to say that Dr. Solly Zuckerman of the British Medical Research Council was coming to see me. This was a pleasant surprise, since I had known Dr. Zuckerman during my medical school days in the early thirties when he was a Fellow in Professor Fulton's department at Yale. Later he became the professor of anatomy at the University of Birmingham. During the war he had been concerned with the analysis of the effects of weapons. The concepts of Standardized Casualty Rate (SCR) and Standardized Killed Rate (SKR) had been developed, terms as cold and gruesome as they sound. It was his mission to learn the SKR and SCR for the atomic bomb. Professor Zuckerman made us familiar with the methods for the calculation. Fundamentally, the SKR is the number killed, assuming a population density of one person per thousand square feet in the area at risk. The latter represents the sum of the products of the fractions killed in each ring zone by the areas of the ring zones. On this basis we ultimately found in Hiroshima that the vulnerable area for the killed was 2.85 square miles, and for all casualties 9.36 square miles. From these data an SKR of 79,450 and an SCR of 260,900 were calculated. This SCR is about 6,500 times as great as for a high-explosive bomb in Britain, assuming a population half in the open and half in British houses. The ratio is approximate because of the dubious assumption that the populations under consideration are comparable. These data ultimately reached the British and the world.

When Colonel Swanson and Professor Bowman's calculations were completed, the painstaking labor of tracing the persons and projecting the plans of the buildings was finally rewarded. It was found that at 250 to 450 meters from the hypocenter (650 to 750 meters from airburst), more than 150 inches of water (5 feet 4 inches of concrete) were needed to protect against death from radiation and more than 250 inches of water and 9 feet of concrete to protect against radiation injury. At 750 meters (960 meters from airburst) more than 50 inches of water were necessary to protect against death, and more than 250 inches of water (nine feet of concrete) against radiation injury. At 1,000 meters (1,165 meters from airburst) more than 3.8 inches of water (1.7 inches of concrete) were required to protect against serious radiation injury. At this distance very few persons who were in concrete structures suffered severe radiation effects. When these calculations had been completed, Dr. Victor Weisskopf of the Massachusetts Institute of Technology, one of the consultants to the Manhattan Project, came to see us in order to determine whether the medical data would correlate with physical estimates of radiation dosage at various distances from the epicenter. He had with him a penciled curve. It was remarkable that the points, supplied on the basis of an assumed LD 50 dose for man, fell rather closely along the curve.

As it neared its end, the tempo of accomplishment in the preparation of the report actually seemed to increase. Some acceleration may have resulted from external stimuli. As September approached my chief at Yale, Dr. M. C. Winternitz, was pointing out with clarity and force that the school year was about to begin. As a last act we prepared a letter for Colonel Oughterson's signature that summarized the major findings, pointed out some directions where further investigation was needed, and most particularly stressed the importance of a continuing study over many years of the population that had been exposed. This letter was addressed to the surgeon generals of the army, navy, and air force, to whom the report was duly transmitted. This recommendation was subsequently referred by the surgeon general of the army to the National Research Council and was in fact the major stimulus for the creation of the Atomic Bomb Casualty Commission that has continued the collaborative effort between Japanese and American scientists that began with the original investigation of 1945.

And so the work was completed almost one year after it was begun. It was the end of many journeys, the end of a taxing challenge and struggle and of an exciting adventure, and the end and the beginning of many searchings of soul.

The use of this weapon, as we contemplated it, and as we saw its effects and wrote of them, filled us with revulsion. We acquired a sympathy, not for those on the periphery who acquired a Prometheus complex and cried *culpa mea* as a means of proclaiming their own importance, but for the physicists who bore the real responsibility for the development of the atomic bomb and who suffered genuine torment of conscience. Were we, even in the aftermath, accessories to a crime against mankind? Surely the death and injury of innocents

A view across the hypocenter, toward the Geibi and Sanwa bank buildings. The wall at the left is a remnant of the Shima Hospital. The upright tree, stripped of branches, indicates the downward direction of the blast at a point very close to the hypocenter. At the right are the shattered walls of the Bankers' Club.

A view comparable to the previous one, showing the city in the process of regrowth, March 1949.

The peace monument at the Chamber of Commerce Building, March 1949.

A view of the Chamber of Commerce Building from the balcony of the Businessmen's Club. The impact of the blast, which buckled the concrete walls, is evident.

A view comparable to the previous one, showing the rebuilding of the city in March 1949. The Chamber of Commerce Building has been left as a memorial of the first atomic bombing.

is wickedness that can never be condoned. But even killing by hand, in combat, while honoring the traditions of "chivalry," is still murder. The crime is of the same kind. Chivalry was crushed and burned when the first unseeing stones and firebrands were hurled. It had died centuries before Hiroshima. We thought also of the 15,000 hospital beds in the Marianas, now never to be used, and of the hundreds of thousands of lives, American and Japanese, that would have been the cost of the assault and conquest of the home islands of Japan. Had more been spared than were lost and maimed in the two cities? But why could not an atomic explosion near, but not upon, a living city, have been as persuasive? Even if it was "necessary" to destroy one city, how could one justify the devastation of another? We could only hope that reasons based on morality as well as strategy dictated the decisions.

When we saw the pitifully crippled and maimed we felt both guilt and shame. But was the absence of resentfulness the stoicism of a brave and disciplined people, or was this also some reflection of guilt on their own part? Perhaps there was an element of both.

But once the deed was done, criminal or salutary, there was clearly a duty to perform, to measure not merely the power of a weapon soon to become outmoded or extinct, but the nature and extent of radiation injury in man. Never before had human beings been exposed en masse to this force that surely would have to be lived with, or even lived by. This power could be harnessed for good although it would always carry a threat. In performing this work, we could then, not merely unthinkingly obey orders, but make a partial and uneasy peace with conscience. While the opportunity was born of tragedy, it was clearly a necessity to make the best use of it. We plunged into the task with an inner compulsion, for we knew that time was running out. The work could surely have been done much better by a team selected in advance and equipped with all the instruments of modern laboratory science. As it was, much less would have been accomplished without the expert knowledge, ingenuity, ideas, and unflagging efforts of our Japanese colleagues.

When, on September 6, 1946, the completed report of some 1,300 pages, bound in six substantial volumes, was handed to Colonel Ash, there ended a still vivid chapter. But while the chapter came to

an end we were left with the uneasy feeling that the book remains un-
finished—and it continues as a haunting memory. May the evil of
which it tells never occur again!